LOOKING GOOD, BUT FEELING BAD

Looking Good, But Feeling Bad

*How a Healthy Body Image Can Set You Free
to Enjoy the Way You Look*

Mary Ann Mayo

Servant Publications
Ann Arbor, Michigan

This book was originaly published under the title *Skin Deep*.

Vine Books is an imprint of Servant Publications especially designed to serve Evangelical Christians.

Published by Servant Publications
P.O. Box 8617
Ann Arbor, Michigan 48107

Cover design by Syncom

94 95 96 97 98   10 9 8 7 6 5 4 3 2 1

Printed in the United States of America

ISBN 0-89283-768-3

Library of Congress Cataloging-in-Publication Data
Mayo, Mary Ann.
 [Skin Deep]
 Looking good, but feeling bad : how a healthy body image can set you free to enjoy the way you look / Mary Ann Mayo
 216 p. cm.
 Includes bibliographical references.
 ISBN 0-89283-867-1
 1. Body, Human—Religious aspects—Christianity. 2. Self-respect—Religious aspects—Christianity. 3. Body image. 4. Self-respect.
5. Christian life—1960– I. Title.
BT741.2.M39 1992
233'.5–dc20
                                                    93-45001

Dedication

*This book is dedicated to former First Lady Barbara Bush,
whose healthy self-image offers a positive role model
in a world where body image reigns supreme.*

Contents

ACKNOWLEDGMENTS

MANY THANKS to my husband, Joe, for diligently finding just the right illustration, and to both he and my daughter, Malika, for putting up with my forgetting to get groceries and losing track of time.

Very special appreciation is directed to David Putnam, whose sensitive writing and challenging conversations gave me a glimpse into the world of the disabled. He provided a depth of understanding I could not have obtained without him.

The Lord has used Fred Chay to challenge me, encourage me, and motivate me to rework chapters when I didn't think I had the energy to do it! Thank you, Fred.

Special appreciation to the wise counsel of Mike Smith, Beth Feia, and Ann Spangler.

Introduction

THERE IS A NEW GOD IN TOWN: the god of physical perfection. Being beautiful and thin or handsome and muscular promises love, happiness, and acceptance. The beautiful people fascinate and mesmerize us. Harboring the feeling that we don't quite measure up, we easily swallow the glittering gospel of physical perfection.

This new god offers a myriad of self-help paths: diets, cosmetic surgery, magical creams, exercise. Dedication and self-discipline guarantee results. Anyone who feels like a square peg can push, shove, and rearrange themselves into the proverbial round hole. Fueled by our fear of imperfection, we pursue anything that promises to improve our appearance.

The god of physical perfection also promises greater self-worth. The media constantly bombards us with messages about how we can adorn or alter our bodies and thereby enhance the quality of our lives. Self-mastery offers a sense of control in a world where we feel increasingly disconnected. The self-improvement industry and the media have significant financial reasons for wanting us to believe in the new god's premise. Just getting rid of wrinkles motivates us to spend about fifty-eight million dollars a week.[1]

But we worship an illusive ideal, one which we can never seem to attain. Beauty is always just out of reach. This new god is a liar. The promises sound good... even healthy. But they don't work. They at first produce the "high" which convinces us we are taking responsibility for ending our unhappiness. Then our new-found hope fades faster than the label on our "just do it" athletic shoes. We may actually look better and be healthier than ever, but continue to feel just as awful.

Despite our most compulsive efforts to be "all that we can be," why do we so often seem to fall short of our goal? From the seeds we sow with such assurance, why do we often reap greater disillusionment and an even more diminished self-concept? Why does all this frenetic effort and determination so frequently fail to produce the promised contentment?

Our problem is an internal one, while this new god offers an external cure. The god of physical perfection promises that the achievement of outer goals will fix what ails us inside. Happiness and success will inevitably follow when we become as "body beautiful" as possible. *Self-improvement has become synonymous with self-acceptance.*

Our efforts at physical perfection offer us tangible solutions to fix what ails us—the newest gym, the latest diet, hip fashions, a nip or tuck here or there. These cures require effort, energy, and money, but actually enable us to avoid the tedious and scary prospect of searching inward. They make us *feel* alive and up-to-date, but keep us from looking into the recesses of our soul. Thus distracted, we can easily continue to deny the trouble inside.

When we opt for secrecy and self-deception, the relentless pain continues to fuel our compulsive patterns of living. We have become a country of addicts. Becoming the best we can be as a route to happiness has tragically backfired. Focusing on the external and ignoring our internal needs have undermined our confidence. Rather than contentment, the result is often increased anxiety.

Ironically, seeking happiness through physical perfection keeps us focused on how we *don't* measure up. We intuitively know that despite our best efforts we will never reflect the image of the models in *Elle.* Even so, we rarely stop to evaluate the value of our headlong pursuit. Instead, we redouble our efforts and rededicate ourselves to working even harder and finding ever more effective procedures, products, and programs. Our unexamined belief that we are on the correct path intensifies our pursuit and blinds us to alternatives that offer a truly healthy self-image.

Even if we give it little conscious thought, body image can affect our lives as profoundly as our faith. Indeed, the pursuit of physical perfection can become a religion. What we think about our bodies and how we believe others view us can determine the course of our lives. Our body image affects our relationships on every level—from the most casual to the most intimate.

What motivates our intense desire for self-improvement? By what criteria are we to critique ourselves and others? Do our automatic assumptions about people really define reality? Unhooking a mindset that equates self-improvement with self-acceptance requires some serious rethinking. We must examine our unconscious maneuverings to live out such an ideology and explore what really needs changing and whether it can be fixed by an external intervention. What alternatives are there?

Looking Good, But Feeling Bad is designed to help you reexamine what you have taken for granted. My hope is that you will be challenged to see yourself and others with new eyes.

THE QUICKSAND OF FASHION

A positive self-image has not always been so clearly determined by meeting the prevailing standards of beauty and accomplishment. In the past, a more common criteria was contentment, an inner peace involving acceptance of who we are based on underlying values and belief systems. The resulting sense of security carried with it a sense of connectedness with others—a family who loved us, honest work, and good friends. In our Western culture, this connectedness most often extended to a God we felt we knew personally.

Today, the emotional wallop we experience in our daily lives is the gauge by which we determine success. Inner worth and happiness is sought through the vicissitudes of fashion and fad—presented as the "easy solution," easier than searching inward for a personal view of life's deepest meaning.

We seek acceptance and self-worth through the application of an external quick fix. But just as a Band-Aid is ineffective on an infected sore, so are self-improvement programs inadequate to soothe an ailing soul. Feeling unacceptable is a *spiritual problem,* requiring a *spiritual solution.*

As psychiatrist Dr. Melvin Kinder observes, "We have lost the truth that human beings should not be improved but should be nurtured."[2] Self-improvement activities inevitably reinforce our inadequacy, whereas nurturing affirms who we are. In our search to feel accepted and lovable, we have chosen a path that has left us depleted rather than restored. We complicate the process of self-acceptance by comparison with others. The resulting envy keeps us from loving others and generating the approval we seek. The "solution" to become the "best" comes at a high cost, alienating us from those whose affirmation we so desire.

Jesus of Nazareth made the same observation: "Love God with all your heart and with all your soul and with all your mind.... Love your neighbor as yourself" (Mt 22:37, 39). This divine physician knew that life has no meaning apart from its largest sense and that love and acceptance are the keys to feeling whole.

The ability to love is dependent on the value people place on themselves. An individual who hates himself or herself is too self-possessed to be able to love another fully. The problem of comparison is also overcome by loving both ourselves and others. Acts of love have the mystical effect of making us feel good and adequate. The ability to love ourselves and others is a far more dependable solution to acceptance than striving to meet societal standards that vary from season to season.

PURSUING PLANS THAT DON'T WORK

Once we reach out and touch a hot pan on the stove, we rarely do it again. But we continue to seek a healthy body image and inner peace through activities that provide only temporary relief. And the worst aspect of the search for happiness through self-improvement is the despair we experience when we fail! We usually conclude that we didn't work hard enough or chose the wrong program.

We often figure we might as well give up: our problems are apparently so severe that no amount of effort will overcome them. Instead of a bolstered self-image, we must come to terms with an even more damaged view of ourselves. In essence, we keep putting our hand on the hot stove!

The effect that body image has on the individual and society is largely ignored. We travel through our days oblivious that we are operating under this powerful force which radically affects the decisions we make about our own lives and others. We are unaware that such an ideology even exists. Often we take its validity for granted.

Perhaps an analogy would be helpful. I spend much of my time teaching and encouraging parents to take responsibility for educating their children about sex. The prevailing belief is that sex education consists of a very awkward talk sometime before a child decides to marry! Without any specific references to sex, parents are actually continually teaching their child what it means to be a sexual person. "Sex education" takes place whether parents participate consciously or not. By observing the interaction of the mother and father, the child learns how men and women are to treat one another. If expressions of affection and touch are severely

limited, conclusions are reached about their appropriate-
ness. Should a parent respond to natural curiosity about the
body with disgust, fearfulness or even greater curiosity can be
aroused.

Our education about body image works much the same
way. We are often unaware of the pressures body image
exerts, the conclusions we make, and the actions we take
accordingly. The view we hold of our own bodies and those
of others deeply influences our choices and friendships, as
well as the judgments we make about life.

"Beautiful people get all the breaks." "Fat people are lazy."
"The disabled are asexual." Such beliefs go unchallenged
and are accepted as true. The encouragement to "be a better
you" sounds healthy and modern. Nothing is wrong with
wanting to look your best. Indeed, most people can legiti-
mately benefit from improving their physical fitness.

The line is fine, however, between healthy self-enhance-
ment and the damaging drive activated by a sense of inadequacy. Consequently, we seldom question the wisdom of
signing up for an extra aerobics class, purchasing a sixty-
dollar eye creme, liposuction for our chin, or another weight-
loss program. But such behaviors and choices can result in
denying our real needs and ignoring the possibility of anything being wrong with our inner life. The quest to "grow"
and "improve" is legitimate. But when the problem is an
inner sense of unacceptability, it is medicine for the wrong
illness.

The false god's mandate that physical perfection will bring
us contentment is accepted at face value. We become so busy
and preoccupied with all that "good, healthy stuff" that we
don't take time to check out whether it really works. Americans typically believe that hard work pays off. We just need
to "keep on keeping on." If one course of action doesn't succeed, we try another. In the end, the pursuit of becoming a
"better" person becomes an end in itself.

An exaggeration? Think about the last time you picked up a magazine because it offered a handy-dandy, quicker-than-ever solution to losing weight, getting in shape, or redesigning an off-center nose. Such a question rarely requires longterm memory! Do you run for the sheer joy of it or are you "training" for a marathon? Are your credit card accounts filled with clothes and cosmetics you can't really afford? Are you always on a diet? Do people say you need to gain weight? Are you determined to benchpress two hundred pounds before Christmas? Have you made an appointment with your dentist to have your teeth bleached or be fitted for invisible braces?

As long as we believe perfection offers an answer to our emptiness and pain, we will continue to pursue any route that promises we can achieve it. We have become a people who spend more time perfecting ourselves than living life! Pity the individual whose goal is to be merely *content*. That person is seen as lacking in vision and drive!

How startling that a nation which is predominately Christian—a faith whose main tenets are grace and love—is as susceptible as any other in seeking validity through appearance. We will examine some of the reasons for our predicament in chapter ten.

HOW TO GET THE MOST OUT OF THIS BOOK

Looking Good, But Feeling Bad is a study of the power of body image. My hope is that as you read, you will become more aware of both the subtle and obvious ways you have been influenced by commonly held myths and truths about body image. You will be challenged to question the validity of the message that self-improvement increases self-acceptance. You will be asked to examine your own decisions regarding the self-improvement merry-go-round we all find ourselves riding.

More and more people are considering spiritual solutions

to fill the void they have been unable to fill any other way. Some soothe the gnawing curse of unacceptability by declaring *themselves* god, à la New Age. Others seek miraculous and instantaneous healing. In most cases, the answer is still being sought through the quick fix rather than the time-consuming, thoughtful, and challenging process of coming to terms with who we are in relation to other people, ourselves, our bodies, and God.

As you read, continually ask yourself what gives you a sense of worth. Is your answer consistent with your behavior? Do you feel part of a larger plan, or is your time and purpose limited to whom you can impress and how you interact within your personal sphere of influence? Is being content and feeling at peace an acceptable goal for you? Or do you find significance in doing something outstanding, in having the perfect body or the right look, or minimally being "the best *you* can be"?

Was there ever a time when contentment was enough for you? When was it? What changed? Are there things about that time you would like to experience again? Even though we can't go back, are there emotional or relational elements that could be reestablished in your life now?

As you ponder the research presented throughout this book, examine the ways you have thought about your body and your abilities. Having been raised in the South, I remember growing up fearful of developing "the big head." Thinking too much of yourself was a sin right up there with stealing and lying. Humility was the acceptable trait, with a little self-deprecation thrown in for good measure.

Like many others, I concluded that if feeling good about yourself was bad, feeling bad about yourself must be good. Having suffered the consequences of feeling bad about myself and having taken time to reexamine my assumptions, I have since learned that a realistic appraisal is true wisdom. A very wise man, the Apostle Paul, says, "Do not think of yourself more highly than you ought, but rather think of yourself with sober judgment…" (Rom 12:3).

Are you realistic about who you are and what you look like? Are you able to evaluate yourself objectively? Have you judged your worth by how you stack up against your neighbor? With whom are you comparing yourself? Are you measuring yourself against a person whose life, build, skin color, or size is unrelated to yours? How did you form the expectations you have for yourself?

Pull out some family pictures and try to remember how you felt at different stages of your life. Take note of the consistencies and look realistically at the genetic factors that identify you with your family. Instead of rejecting the history of who you are, make the choice to absorb and accept your unique inheritance.

Perhaps such questions make you feel a little overwhelmed. Others may feel a bit smug, feeling that they have based their body image on what they consider a firmer foundation than looks. As you read on, new insights and awareness will occur. As much as possible, don't dismiss them as just interesting facts without first reviewing the meaning they hold for you. You will be helped in the process by the reflections and questions at the end of most of the chapters.

In truth, the peace of mind that comes with self-acceptance is the fruit not so much of *transformation into a new self* as much as the fruit of *reclaiming parts of our old self.* May your reclamation be a joyous one which brings you contentment.

Part One

This Sacred Garment

*The body is a sacred garment. It's your first and last garment;
it is what you enter life in and what you depart life with, and
it should be treated with honor.* **Martha Graham, 1895-1991**

1

Beauty Is in the Eye of the Beholder

*B*ATHED IN COOL fluorescent light, the tubes and stainless steel stand out in stark contrast with the warm vitality enclosed in the isolettes. Each healthy bundle of life already has a distinct personality, despite their having been in the outer world a mere few hours.

The nurses carefully adjust the tiny body in the isolette nearest the window. A little bow announces, "I'm a girl," with a pink blanket to complete the picture. Amy's delicate little lips win the praises of the nurses. The family remarks that "she looks just like Aunt Helene"—which means she is bound to be beautiful and enjoy her share of male attention. Amy's mother considers her daughter special. She vows to be there for her, protecting her, loving her, making sure she will grow up healthy and happy. Surely this child deserves her mother's undivided attention. Happy with her decision to end her job last month, she is sure her days as a mother are going to be full of special joy.

One row over lies all six pounds, six ounces of Dan's active little body. His tiny hands reach into the air—opening and closing, grasping, and stretching for contact with anything that might seem more familiar than this waterless aquarium.

23

Something pretty awful just catapulted him from the warmth and security of his last two hundred and sixty-seven days into this bright, hard place. Dan registers his protest with loud cries. Maybe if he keeps it up, he might be mysteriously transported back to the warm spot that had felt so familiar and safe.

Farther over, near the wall, is Tiffany. She arrived on time, despite the premature contractions that had started early in her mother's pregnancy. Her dad had missed the delivery—his sales meeting a once-in-a-lifetime opportunity. But he was there now, appropriately "oohing" and "ahhing" outside the glass and motioning the nurse to move his baby girl closer. Tiffany's mom was proud her daughter had all the requisite toes and fingers. She was even moved by the little tuft of red hair that already curled on her forehead. Just like me, she thought.

Three wonderful beginnings, three magnificent potentials, three hopeful possibilities for president of the United States or some such grand accomplishment. Three kids from ordinary middle-class parents whose intentions were loving and good and sincere. Three sets of parents vitally concerned for the welfare of their newborns.

Why then, twenty-four years later, is Amy moving to a new state that allows her the possibility of marrying her female lover? Why then, did Dan celebrate his latest birthday out of work—scrambling for a new place to live, having been evicted from his last home because of his inability to keep drugs out of his life? Why then, has Tiffany's life been punctuated by painful episodes of bulimia? Why had she just rejected the marriage offer of a decent and loving young man—whom she loves?

Why indeed? Did their parents fail them? Did society victimize them? Did the media corrupt them? Did their early life experience create unrealistic expectations? Did their own inherent selfishness create havoc? What happened between the bright hopes of the hospital nursery and the grim reality of adult life? Let's analyze these three cases for some possible answers.

AMY

Amy's mother had been raised in a rather large extended family. Until the age of seven, her life had been an idyllic interplay of cooking with the women, romping with her dog, and exploring the world of castles and princes through books. Her world changed rapidly, however, when her father accepted a job in another state. The family relocated, along with her grandfather. Amy's mom was left in his care while her mother and father busied themselves with their new community. Sadly, the grandfather began a slow seduction of the lonely little girl that continued until his death seven years later.

Having vowed to protect any child she ever brought into the world, Amy's mother attempted to control everything that went on in her daughter's life. She was constantly carried, never left with babysitters, and cautioned against potential dangers that seemed to lurk around every corner. By school age, Amy was a fearful child whose normal growth toward autonomy had been severely thwarted. She feared separation from her parents and dared not try anything on her own. One of her earliest memories involved an incident on the playground when she wanted to join a group of children. She was prevented by firm grasps on her little arms by both parents, who told her that joining the neighborhood kids was inappropriate.

Along with a poor sense of her individuality, her isolation from the "dangerous world" produced intense pressure on Amy to conform. She felt small, asexual, undifferentiated. Like other children who remain merged with their parents, she experienced her body as somehow separate from herself and easily invaded by others.

Going off to college was traumatic for Amy, but her mother was convinced the proper, girls' school was a safe choice. This young woman attempted to gain a sense of her boundaries through vigorous exercise and frequent refusal to eat. Interestingly, Amy felt further defined when she discovered the effect she had on men. Her dress and manner became somewhat exhibitionist, although her reputation was "all words, no action."

During her second semester, Amy was the victim of a date rape. Feeling vulnerable and incapable of protecting herself, she redoubled her efforts at exercise and dove deeper into her anorexic behavior. Amy found sympathetic ears along with a sense of protection and strength through her involvement with the women's activist movement on campus. Their support and fellowship enabled her to break her unhealthy eating patterns. She gained a feeling of control over her life through strong identification with the more radical feminists. Before long, Amy was sexually involved with another woman. Her safety, after all, had always been found in the arms of a woman.

DAN

Dan's early years were pretty typical. Brothers and sisters, a middle-class neighborhood, and loving but busy parents all enabled Dan to feel pretty good about himself. Granted, he was on the small side, the brunt of frequent remarks at school. But Dan was a good student and no one was quicker or a better kicker on the soccer field. He had found his niche.

At fourteen Dan was riding in a car with a group of friends when the inexperienced driver overcorrected around a curve. The car rolled three times. One person was killed and others suffered broken bones. Dan had been catapulted through the air and hit a wire fence, which severely cut his face and severed his right ear.

Despite a series of plastic surgeries, Dan was left with a deep scar across his face and a prosthetic ear. His friends called him S.F.—short for Scarface. In a misguided attempt to play down the significance of Dan's false ear, his family began a series of jokes on the wonder of a removable ear.

"One hundred and one things to do with a false ear" became a favorite topic at the dinner table.

Research done by J. Kevin Thompson from the University of South Florida indicates that Dan's injury occurred at a particularly vulnerable time in his life.[1] Teasing between the ages of eight and sixteen is most likely to leave long-lasting effects, particularly if it comes from parents, teachers, coaches, or other authority figures. Such children often grow up with greater dissatisfaction with their body and tend to suffer tremendous loss of self-esteem that results in depression.

In order to hide his scar and ear, Dan let his hair grow long and full. No longer willing to take the razzing on the soccer field, he began to associate with others who were frequently the brunt of unkind remarks and who seemed less discriminating in their acceptance. Since many of those kids escaped their pain through drugs, it wasn't long until Dan joined them.

His depression was debilitating. Dan alternated between withdrawing and being tough and rejecting, making sure he did to others before they did to him. Much to his parents dismay, he acquired several tattoos. They reflected his anger and demonstrated his alienation, while also giving Dan some sense of boundaries as to his identity. Somehow he made it through high school despite his erratic attendance, then bounced from job to job, rehab to rehab.

TIFFANY

It wasn't that Tiffany's mom and dad didn't love her. Whenever they went on business trips, her pictures lined their briefcases. There was just never enough time... especially for parents who both pursued high-powered careers.

Tiffany's mother insisted that fresh flowers always grace their house. She despised getting her hands dirty and wet, so a full-time gardener did the "dirty" work. The same was true in relating to Tiffany. Her mother seemed to enjoy her as long as she was sweet and pleasant, but dealing with "dirty" work—like changing diapers, feeding, and burping—were tasks to be endured or passed on to someone else.

From birth Tiffany's natural bodily processes were dealt with as quickly and efficiently as possible. There were no leisurely baths, no time of kicking freely without the bulk of diapers. Even though her mother nursed the baby for the first few weeks, Tiffany was expected to do her business within a specified time. "Mothers were not meant to be human pacifiers," her mother told her friends.

By age two, Tiffany learned that her grubby hugs caused immeasurable problems for her mother's dry-cleaned clothes. So she stopped hugging. The string of nannies did their perfunctory duty in touching and caring for Tiffany, but the primary message she received was that she was not wanted. Something was wrong. No one liked to touch her or derived joy from her little body.

Like all newborns, Tiffany had been incapable of distinguishing her body from anyone else's. Body image develops more clearly as a child grows. Body boundaries are discovered after the first few months. Between eight and thirteen months, a child begins to consider objects as existing apart from their immediate perception.

Slowly Tiffany understood that there was space beyond her body, but full imaging was not developed until she was eighteen months old. She began to think of something or someone without an immediate cue. Her ability to say "no" verified her growing sense of who she was, but that person was not quite whole.

Deprived of warm and loving touch, Tiffany was unable to use such contact as a source of reference for her body image. Consequently, her view of herself was distorted, shapeless, blurry. She perceived herself to be heavy—a common conclusion of people with similar upbringing. She adapted by wearing loose clothes and began a cycle of bingeing and purging.

As she matured, Tiffany received several beauty honors, a fact she easily dismissed. Her mirror reflected a woman who was unattractive and, therefore, unworthy. Her self-concept had little to do with reality. In order to make up for her perceived undesirability, Tiffany sought to be perfect in other ways. An excellent student, she graduated second in her nursing class.

From an outsider's vantage point, Tiffany was beautiful, in control, and smart. But try as she might, she simply didn't measure up in her own eyes. When Greg asked Tiffany to marry him, she felt she had to end the relationship. What did a wonderful man like Greg need with a woman who raided the refrigerator as soon as he dropped her off and then spent the rest of the evening throwing up?

Tiffany sought help through her pastor. Praying together for healing didn't seem to help any. How could she accept God's unconditional love when she couldn't even believe Greg truly wanted to marry her?

UNDERSTANDING BODY IMAGE

Granted, the factors that shape human life are many and complex. Yet our three babies grew up to be filled with sorrow and unhappiness. They pursued or avoided relationships and made both short-term and permanent decisions based, in part, on their body image.

The definition of body image has been eluding scientists since the early 1930s when they observed brain-damaged patients whose perception of themselves was altered by their medical problems. Paul Schilder authored *The Image and Appearance of the Human Body*, in which he sought an expansive definition that encompassed everything from organic pathology to one's symbolic emotional concepts of self. More recent researchers, frustrated by the compartmentalization of the field, have been pushing for distinctions in understanding body image along the following lines:

1. An object in space that moves and responds to stimuli.
2. A person's comprehension of the body and how it functions.
3. A person's emotionally charged notions or value of the body.[2]

Clearly, body image is more than we see in the mirror! It includes everything from the body as it really is (and who can be the judge of that?) to the body as it is perceived in an emotionally charged system of personal values. Perhaps you awoke this morning feeling energized and ready to go about your business. You felt rested, your muscles seemed in good tone, there was a spring in your step. You looked in the mirror and liked what you saw. Sure, there were a few more gray hairs, but no new wrinkles! Everyone thought your new hairstyle took years off your age. It seemed a great day to bring out that new outfit, shirt, or tie. You stood extra tall as you walked into work.

Then you were introduced to the firm's newest employee. You are convinced this college grad didn't really get out of a rumpled bed this morning. That young twirp must have stepped right off the pages of the latest fashion magazine. Suddenly, your shoulders droop, your chest contracts, and your mouth is transformed from its loving and friendly smile to a pair of hard-edged lips. Dejectedly walking back to your office, you become aware of a new catch in your hip; the reflection in the glass reveals an old and tired person. Is that really you? What happened in a mere forty-five minutes?

Body image is based more on feeling than fact.[3] As Tiffany demonstrated, all the beauty contests in the world and all the accolades of friends could not change her image of herself as fat and unattractive. Some individuals who seek cosmetic surgery are clearly less than realistic about their perceived imperfections. Although exceptions can be found, especially among the disabled, studies indicate that the vast majority of people underestimate their attractiveness and typically misinterpret other's reactions to them.

Body image is influenced by many factors. When you went into work feeling so good, only to be deflated within minutes, you were processing a number of facets of body experiences. You took with you your perception and attitude toward how you looked, your sense of body size and the position it occupies in space, your consciousness of body boundaries and capabilities, and your sense of yourself as a male or female. Your body image consisted not only of your view of your attractiveness, but also awareness of sensations and a sense of your body's function, fitness, and health.

Not everything you were perceiving was on a conscious level. Perhaps you were unaware that the new employee reminded you of your own son or daughter, thus eliciting fears of getting old and becoming less capable and in control. Perhaps you were only dimly conscious that you felt intimidated by his or her being four inches taller than you.

Body image is part of who we think we are. Dan compensated for his short stature by finding activities that didn't require bulk and size. But the facial scar and loss of his ear changed his perception of himself. It wasn't just that he was disfigured. Dan suddenly felt disqualified from living life normally. Amy's sense of vulnerability convinced her she needed protection that could be provided only by others. The sense of self, of who we are, is always interwoven with the image of one's body.

Most women and now increasing numbers of men, use cosmetics to enhance their attractiveness or improve imperfect features. Women typically choose clothes that maximize their best features and minimize the size of overly large breasts or big hips. Men may select a red or yellow "power" tie when they want to appear especially forceful. It isn't difficult to think of several activities or choices made as a result of beliefs we hold about our body image.

I am fast approaching my fiftieth birthday. Surprisingly, I see it as a rather positive milestone. Perhaps it helps that writing and counseling are two rare professions in which a woman supposedly becomes more competent with age! But this upcoming milestone has made me aware of some changing attitudes I have toward my body. After years of maintaining a stick-thin figure, I now find myself more comfortable with a few additional pounds. Carrying a few extra fat cells has become less important to me than feeling more "substantial." I enjoy being in good condition, despite minor aches and pains. I feel healthy and solid, suddenly preferable to looking model-perfect. A psychologist would probably remind me that I've merely adjusted to the reality of entering my "mature" years. Perhaps so. Still, I like it.

That my body image is changing is normal and natural. Throughout life we make nips and tucks in our perception of ourselves. Body image is never completely fixed and is always subject to revision. Perhaps you've experienced this on a day when getting out of bed was a major chore. You wanted to put on a pair of sweats—preferably black and definitely oversized—but instead you forced yourself to pick out the cheeriest thing in your closet. Interestingly, the strategy worked. The world looked brighter and so did you.

Studies tell us that slow changes are much easier to adjust to than abrupt ones. This is probably true for everyone except teenagers, who feel their metamorphosis is happening under the magnifying lens of the whole world! Plastic surgeons report that, despite pleasing results, patients sometimes need time to adjust and incorporate their new image.

Body image is influenced by other people. By the age of two, most toddlers can recognize themselves in the mirror. But what they see and how they feel about that image has been affected by the type of caretaking they have received since birth. In the past decade we have seen the rise of therapies that focus on the nurturing one received as a child. The research done in relation to these therapies attests to the significance of the need for quality care of the young. Later life is always related to earlier life, particularly concerning issues of acceptance and fears of abandonment.

In addition to early caretaking experiences, people receive reactions throughout their lives in terms of their attractiveness, masculinity or femininity, their physical strength, and even racial stereotypes. A survey done by the Metropolitan Chicago Information Center suggests that "African-Americans are more likely than whites to hold negative opinions of their fellow blacks' innate capabilities."[4] Seventy-six percent of black preschoolers in one study chose a black doll as being the "bad" one. Researchers reveal that when black children are asked whether they want to play with a black or white doll, sixty to seventy-eight percent will select the white doll.

Body image affects what we do with the information we gather from the world. Dan concluded that everyone reacted to the scar on his face. The world became a hostile place from which to escape. The matron with a face-lift becomes preoccupied with making mental notes of her friend's surgery and what might have been done differently for her. The boy who grows up with a disproportionate nose spends inordinate amounts of time comparing and considering what life would be like if his nose were more "normal." Perhaps that little red-haired girl in the third row would ask for his phone number! Men who are balding become conscious of other men's balding patterns, perhaps concluding that they were passed over for the latest promotion because they are looking old. Such self-consciousness inevitably sets up situations in which what is expected to be seen is seen.

Body image affects our behavior. Hypochondriacs distort their perception of the body through imaginary illness. The message they have received is, "there is something basically wrong with me." Similarly, self-mutilating adolescents have become so alienated from their "gross, contaminated" body that laceration becomes an appropriate expression of self-hatred.

What we think of our bodies—whether consciously, subconsciously, or unconsciously—activates self-fulfilling prophecies about how successful we will be in our interactions with others. A good-looking man, for example, goes into his business meeting feeling assured about himself. His attitude is reinforced by the positive reactions of his co-workers to his attractiveness. They expect his work to be competent and successful and their belief in him further increases the odds of accomplishment.

Conversely, individuals who are unattractive—particularly those with disfigurement of the face, like Dan—become very self-conscious. They tend to speak less, limit their social situations, or practice other socially restricting behaviors that decreases the odds of performing with skill and confidence.

Body image includes integration of the spiritual. This one final observation of body image needs to be addressed. Tiffany's pastor understood that her basic problem was a sense of worthlessness. He pointed out that as a child of God, her life had purpose, meaning, and significance. God's valuation of her is not dependent on the currently popular body type, but based on an unchangeable standard of unconditional love. Having experienced life as a competition, Tiffany struggled with a God who simply loved her as she was. Dan not only felt unworthy, he was angry. What kind of God would allow his life to be ruined by a shattered face?

Amy struggled with her sexual preference. She was particularly confused about how her desire to have children fit in with her lifestyle. She knew other women who had used artificial insemination, or some who had made pacts of convenience with gay men who wanted to father children. Somehow Amy wasn't comfortable with any of those options. Just why was she made sexual anyway? What kind of God would want her to sleep with the enemy? Amy's attempts to clarify such questions had been met with such harsh judgment that simply putting them out of her mind seemed a lot safer. But still, she wondered.

WHERE DO WE GO FROM HERE?

We have taken a brief look at a number of themes that are found in the scientific literature as well as in our own personal experience of body image.

- Body image is based more on feeling than fact.
- Body image is influenced by many factors.
- Body image is part of who we think we are.
- Body image is influenced by other people.
- Body image affects our behavior.
- Body image includes integration of the spiritual.

Throughout the remainder of this book, these truths will be revealed as a common thread woven through the intricacies of people's experience with their bodies. We will explore body image and its effect on sexual relationships, on how we feel about being male and female, on the way people eat, and even the lengths people go to to alter their bodies.

Along the way you will be asked to look at your own life in an effort to understand how body image affects the choices you make. You will continually be challenged to stop and think about the reasons behind the choices you make to look and feel good. Are you motivated by a desire to improve and grow, or are your efforts aimed at overcoming a sense of deficiency? Finally, we will take a look at people who cope in spite of the condition of their bodies.

Many of life's difficulties are connected to the attitudes we hold about how important the body is to success, or conversely, our misguided attempts to deny its significance and power. Tiffany, Dan, and Amy made lifestyle decisions in an effort to apply external solutions to internal problems. Their choices increased their anxiety, left them chronically dissatisfied, exhausted emotionally, and with a damaged self-image. Paradoxically, all their efforts took them further away from a belief in their own worth.

Can you identify with this dilemma? What should we use as criteria for estimating the worth of ourselves and others? What is the attitude we are to hold toward the body?

2

What's Hot, What's Not

*T*HERE SHE WAS, second from the right, her dark hair swinging rhythmically to the music. The lemon yellow leotard revealed a body with absolutely no extra fat, but still subtly curvaceous. It too was swinging. I squirmed in my chair. That was my daughter up on the stage, putting her all into the high school play's dance scene with six other gyrating classmates. I began to giggle, covered my eyes momentarily, and acted, in my daughter's terminology, "decidedly uncool."

I was flooded with memories of a pretty, delicate, little girl who—it could no longer be denied—was fast becoming a ravishing young woman. Perhaps it was the undeniable sensuousness that she innocently exuded, or the juxtaposition of the child/woman in the same body. Whatever it was, I was flooded with mixed emotions.

Shortly thereafter, Malika was off to Spain for summer vacation. That culture included two-hour dinners served at ten each night. Many of the foods were fried and everything tasted delicious. When Malika returned in the fall, what had still lingered of the little girl had been replaced by full-blown womanhood. The combination of late-night eating and normal hormonal changes had transformed my daughter.

Malika didn't like the change one bit. She immediately launched on the typical teen diet that had always worked before: cutting out regular eating and living on junk food! This time it didn't work. Her dad and I argued that Malika looked fine and that most of what she was perceiving as fat was a developed woman's body. Our protests were received with the assertion that she wanted her "little-girl body back," with more bizarre attempts at dieting.

A pattern developed. Malika began cycles of skipping meals followed by ravenous binges. Always neatly dressed, her wardrobe changed to cut-off sweats and oversize tee shirts. One year later she was still refusing to go through her closet or go shopping for new clothes. A week before her senior class cruise, a bathing suit had still not been found.

Obviously, Malika is caught up in the same cultural pressure typical of her peers: the pressure to be thin and thus, beautiful. But she struggles with other pressures as well, more subtle and complex. Becoming an adult with an adult body means having to cope with these realities.

TO BE BEAUTIFUL IS GOOD, TO BE UGLY IS BAD[1]

The idea that there are benefits and payoffs as a result of being beautiful goes back a long way. We can find an example over two thousand years old in the biblical story of Abram and Sarai. Abram understood that beauty was an advantage and could result in favorable treatment. So when he realized Pharaoh was eyeing his beautiful wife Sarai, Abram claimed she was his sister. "[Pharaoh] treated Abram well for her sake, and Abram acquired sheep and cattle, male and female donkeys, menservants and maidservants, and camels" (Gn 12:16). Perhaps this story is the precursor to the modern-day beauty pageant, financial windfall for "Miss Tiny Tot" to "Miss Universe."

The beautiful seem to get all the breaks—an observation most of us have already made. Rarely do we question the validity of such a judgment. Some suggest the preference for the beautiful is inborn, perhaps related to survival. In one study done with infants, two screens were placed on either side of the crib—one displaying an attractive adult, the other an unattractive one. Babies positioned themselves to look at the screen with the attractive face.[2]

If you are good-looking, odds are increased that others will view you as being happier and more successful. You will be seen as smarter and unquestionably more interesting than the "plain Jane" one desk over. Fellow workers describe you as warmer, more poised, and more sociable. All in all, both men and women perceive you as being outgoing, likable, happy, confident, and well-adjusted.

The opposite conclusions are made about "plain Jane." If Jane is in actuality warm, poised, sociable, and happy, she is going to have to work through the stereotype before she will be perceived that way. Once she has already established herself, this will probably not be much of a problem. But what if she interviews for a new job or is in a social setting where she doesn't know anyone?

President Roosevelt and his entourage understood this reality. Acclaimed by history as one of our most admired and capable presidents, in 1921 Roosevelt became paralyzed from the waist down after a bout with polio. He was still a young man, only thirty-nine years old. He spent the next seven years mostly out of sight, convalescing.

Roosevelt was elected president in 1932, despite the fact he could only stand with the aid of braces for short periods. In all his years in the White House, we possess only two pictures of him in a wheelchair. He was never seen lifted or carried even though this was the only way he could get around. Roosevelt sat in regular sturdy chairs from which he could push up. Strong men, who tactfully learned to support his body weight without appearing to do so, were regularly by his side. A cane supplied additional support. To maneuver stairs, Roosevelt bent his elbows and was carried—a stance that required tremendous upper-body strength, but from a distance gave the appearance he was managing on his own.[3]

His wife, Eleanor, defied the odds of the myth that beauty is good by doing good. But throughout her life detractors commented on her "horsey" look and how "homely" she was. When asked if there was anything about her life she regretted, this accomplished woman replied, "I wish I had been prettier."

Press reports support a similar phenomenon occurring with Prince Charles and Lady Diana. Try as he might to be taken seriously for his concerns about the environment and his interest in post-war London architecture, Prince Charles stands at a serious disadvantage. As soon as Di appears on the scene, attention and press reports focus on her. What is beautiful is good… and apparently, immensely more interesting!

LOOKS AND SELF-ESTEEM

We live in a society which prides itself on equality. We may find it uncomfortable to think that because an individual is good-looking, people will presume he or she is also happier, more successful, smarter, more interesting, warmer, and more poised.[4] But they do. And what other people think—especially those who are important to us like parents, friends, and people we admire—is very significant.

If we are unattractive, our friends and family may assume we won't have as much going for us as our stunning sister or handsome brother. The way we look at ourselves and the world is bound to be affected by their reactions. Our choice of friends will most likely be influenced by whether or not they are on our same level of attractiveness. Our looks can even determine who we come in contact with.

Many studies confirm the link between body image and self-esteem.[5] But it is important to remember that *body image is not limited to some conscious picture of what we think we look like.* The image a person holds of his or her body includes not only the condition and visual impact of the body, but also collective attitudes, feelings, and fantasies—only some of which a person consciously realizes. Positive feelings about appearance, fitness, and health lead to healthy psychological adjustment.[6]

So, are attractive people really all that others think they are? Surprisingly, many are. After all, they have received more affirmative social reinforcement than a Plain Jane or John for the exact same behaviors. People have been anxious to please and to cooperate with them.[7] At work, all else being equal, the attractive job applicant will receive the promotion. When their work is evaluated, they enjoy a greater chance of receiving a positive report.[8]

Preferential treatment goes a long way toward creating successful individuals. Have you ever caught yourself reacting differently toward a salesperson or a complaint clerk because of their appearance? It happens all the time.

In one experiment, male college students who believed they were speaking to a pretty young woman (whom they couldn't actually see), chose to use words and manners in the conversation that were different than when they *thought* they were speaking to a plain or unattractive woman. The women to whom they were speaking responded accordingly.[9] Conversations with the unattractive woman ranged from non-responsive to rejecting, undermining the development of social skills and favorable self-concept. The encouragement needed to develop social confidence and competent behavioral patterns are frequently reserved for the good-looking.

Experimenters asked for an evaluation of essays identified as being written by an attractive or unattractive male or female. They found the essays were considered better written if the author was reputed to be good-looking.[10] Studies with personnel directors indicate attractiveness and height, up to a point, are equated with competence.[11] If all this makes you want to run to your therapist for help and affirmation, forget it. Even therapists give better treatment and more personal attention to the better-looking, which enables them to get well faster![12]

As a consequence of all of this, unattractive people are at greater risk for psychological disorders in general, but especially those involving interpersonal conflict and anxiety. Fear of social rejection is increased.[13] Some less attractive people find it difficult not to succumb to the self-fulfilling prophecy that suggests they are what they and others *think* they are.

Poor self-esteem is almost always a factor in psychological problems and is linked to poor body image. There are few solid links between overt mental illness and appearance. Several studies, however, have suggested that people who were diagnosed as having a biogenetic propensity to schizophrenia were judged less attractive.[14]

We might not like to think that we judge people by the way they look. Yet physical characteristics can be related to personality, and therefore we tend to make judgments about people from what is seen. Any good therapist or salesperson will tell you that a person's body does, to some extent, reflect his or her personality make-up. Our physical appearance and our sex are the most obvious facts upon which others have to make decisions about us. First impressions are important.

STRICTLY FEMININE

Today's magazines and television reinforce that women are to be beautiful, slim, and fit.[15] The message is powerful: *it takes a great body to be successful.* Despite living in a world in which women are taking their place in the workplace as equal contributors, success for a female often requires having men find her attractive. The media rarely suggests that being desirable has much to do with competence or intelligence. The emphasis is on having the idealized body.

Such an unrealistic standard inevitably takes its toll and is in part responsible for the higher rate of weight problems and body image distortions seen in the last fifty years. Being overweight in our society is correlated with feelings of isolation, depression, dissatisfaction, failure, and unattractiveness.[16] Pressure to match the slim ideal comes as much from other women as men. In fact, women are *more* apt than men to judge a woman or presume something about her based upon her shape alone.[17]

Since aspects of physical appearance are dynamic and created when people interact with one another, women tend to be sensitive to the impact of cosmetics and clothing. Those classified as *high self-monitors* are especially aware of the effect they have on others in a social setting. They recognize that to a degree they can control their social and self-image.

Such women who also tend to be extroverts will use cosmetics to achieve the social attention and approval they seek. What she does with make-up, how carefully she applies it, and how much she uses is dependent on the context. So too, choice of clothing has been aptly called a "mood altering substance" because of the impact it has on others and ourselves. For example, the woman who wants to impress someone who is known as a male chauvinist would be wise to dress more moderately.

Women who are *low self-monitors* are less sensitive or concerned with the effect they have on others and will tend to wear the same make-up whatever the situation. Some studies link use of cosmetics with positive body image, feelings of social confidence, and a sense of effectiveness.[18] Perhaps what is really being measured is how much a woman has accepted and succeeded in adopting societal standards.

Grooming behaviors are motivated by the desire to manage or control what others think of us, and in turn what we think about ourselves. Many years ago when I was hired to teach at a local community college, I suddenly became interested in growing long fingernails. My desire was directly related to my need to be seen as feminine despite my new career out of the home.

Lynn, a "Cosmo Makeover" in the July 1991 issue of *Cosmopolitan*, discovered becoming a high self-monitor changed her life. She gushes, "... it all takes time but it absolutely transforms me—physically and emotionally! To be honest, I feel good about myself for the first time in my life and find myself gravitating toward mirrors and windows—anything that lets me see my new reflection!"[19] Lynn goes on to state how she is offered seats on the subway, no longer has to pay for drinks, and has become a flirt.

All it took to transform Lynn was "false eyelashes, eye shadow, foundation, bright lip color, and lip pencil." I must say it makes me question all those years I spent learning how to help people in college. Maybe I should have gone to cosmetology school instead! Lynn seems unaware that women tend to overestimate their attractiveness with make-up and underestimate it without.

STRICTLY MASCULINE

Ninety-three percent of women report they attempt to affect their appearance; a none too paltry eighty-two percent of men admit to thinking about or trying to improve their looks.[20] More and more men are using cosmetics and undergoing cosmetic surgery procedures. Not surprisingly, their motivation for self-improvement has to do with how it will affect them occupationally, and secondarily, how appealing it will make them to the opposite sex.

Whether they actively do anything about it or not, almost all men express concern about one aspect of their looks: losing their hair. Hair replacements, tonics, and "miracle" cures for balding have produced a thriving business for many years. And with good reason. Balding men almost universally attempt to detract from or minimize hair loss.

In a recent episode of *The Simpsons*, the father sought help for his baldness by using a new topical medication named "Rogain," which in real life has had some success in stimulating hair growth in young men whose hair is beginning to thin. In the television portrayal, Homer Simpson finds himself with a completely new head of hair. The results are dramatic. He is immediately energized; his neighbors treat him with new respect; even his lovemaking is improved. At work, Homer is promoted to a managerial position and his boss is enraptured with his increasingly creative and successful ideas.

The story ends when Homer is no longer able to use the product and quickly becomes bald again. His confidence shot, he is encouraged by a friend that he is the same man with or without hair. When Homer attempts to communicate his innovative problem-solving techniques to co-workers, they trickle out of the conference room mumbling disparaging remarks. "What would a bald man have to say that we could use, anyway?" "Man, I can't relate to that old geezer." Homer is only moderately comforted by his wife's assurance that she still loves him as much as ever.

Is this fiction? Studies indicate that balding men generally make a less favorable impression. They are perceived as less physically attractive and are assumed to have less desirable personal and interpersonal characteristics. On top of all that, they are thought to be older than they really are.[21] Perhaps the writer or producer of that episode of *The Simpsons* had first-hand experience!

When a man becomes obsessed with his hair loss, more serious psychological problems can develop. One famous TV star reputedly undergoes painful daily electronic treatments, massages, and no longer takes showers for fear the pounding water will damage his remaining locks. Many balding men may have a more negative body image, but are very similar to others in terms of basic self-concept and personality function.[22]

"HARD BODIES, MARSHMALLOWS, AND HUNKS"

One of the oldest attempts to pigeonhole people was done in the forties by W.H. Sheldon.[23] He argued that stereotypical behavioral and personality traits were associated with each of three body types: *mesomorphic, endomorphic, and ectomorphic.* A recent study verified the stability of Sheldon's conclusions over time, with one exception. A greater number of people attributed more positive traits to the thinner body type—the ectomorph—and identified it as the one they would most like to emulate, especially women.[24]

Those who are neither excessively fat or thin are *mesomorphs*, a body type associated with strength, happiness, and dominance. The greatest number of positive behavioral characteristics are attributed to mesomorphs, such as competence, friendship, health, happiness, and intelligence. About the only negative association is with aggression.

Thin *ectomorphs* were originally expected to be on the nervous side and more socially withdrawn. Not too withdrawn, apparently. Work done in 1989 identified thin people as the most sexually appealing and as having the most dates. One can surmise television and other media have had something to do with this shift!

The *endomorph* is a person with a heavy build, viewed in the forties as socially aggressive, lazy, and unattractive. Not much has changed. People with heavy builds are still viewed as being the sloppiest dressers, highly stressed, and the most likely to be depressed. Endomorphs are not expected to be professional or to stand up for themselves. Another rather contradictory stereotype of the obese is that of being "jolly," an expectation best personified by Santa Claus.

According to a Gallup survey conducted for *American Health Magazine* in 1988, there is some discrepancy between what men and women think the opposite sex desires.[25]

Women think men prefer them skinny. The younger the man, the more chance that is true, but overall, sixty-five percent of men say their ideal woman is of *average* body type. Although average size breasts are considered most attractive, males clearly admire large busts. The meaning and significance women's breasts hold for a man is quite subjective.[26]

Men prefer women with a "soft" body look—fifty-nine percent to twenty-seven percent—over the new "hard" body recently coming into fashion. Increasing numbers of women are opting for strength and rejecting the "marshmallow" look they know men prefer. The hard body is especially appealing to the well-educated woman: sixty-five percent of that group prefer it compared to twenty-seven percent of women without a college degree. Sociologists speculate that the shift to fitness among women may reflect increased health consciousness or may be another attempt (as the anorexic look could be interpreted) to downplay femininity. A woman who must compete in a man's world may feel disadvantaged because of her sex and perhaps feel she needs to be muscular to compete.[27]

Many men wish they resembled the cultural ideals of masculinity such as Rambo or the Marlboro Man, but most women report they are happy with medium builds. Men's ideals help them feel satisfied with their weight, while those of women make them feel pressured to lose weight. What we actually are and what the opposite sex prefers is not as far off as what we *think* is desired and expected of us.

HOW WE ARE... HOW WE WANT TO BE[28]

The following charts (pages 48 and 49), compiled from the Gallup poll results, graphically illustrate the way it is from the way we think it is.

The Average Man:
5'10", 172 pounds
38-inch waist
medium width shoulders and chest
Hairy or smooth chest
Lean build
Brown eyes
Short, straight, dark hair
Tanned or untanned
Clean-shaven

Men Want to Be:
5'10", 171 pounds
33-inch waist,
Medium-to-broad shoulders and chest
Hairy or smooth chest
Muscular build
Brown or blue eyes
Short, straight, dark hair
Tanned
Clean-shaven

Men Think Women Want a Man:
6', 173 pounds
32-inch waist
Broad shoulders and chest
Hairy chest
Muscular build
Blue eyes
Short, curly, dark hair
Tanned
Clean-shaven

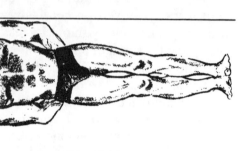

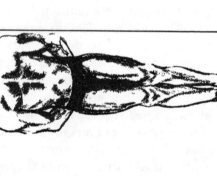

Woman Actually Want a Man:
5'11", 171 pounds
33-inch waist
Medium-to-broad shoulders and chest
Hairy chest
Muscular build
Brown or blue eyes
Short, curly, dark hair
Tanned
Clean-shaven

The Average Woman:
Dress size 10 to 12
5' 3½", 134 pounds
Average-sized breasts
Average body type
Soft body tone
Brown eyes
Short, straight,
dark hair
Some wrinkles,
blemishes, or
freckles,
Untanned

Women Want to Be:
Dress size 8
5' 4", 123 pounds
Average-sized breasts
Average body type
Muscular body tone
Brown or blue eyes
Brown hair, wavy
or curly
Smooth,
tanned skin

Women think Men Want a Woman:
Dress size 8
5' 4", 118 pounds
Large breasts
Thin body type
Soft body tone
Blue eyes
Long, wavy, blond hair
Smooth,
tanned skin

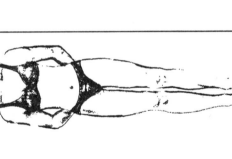

Men Actually Want a Woman:
5' 4", 121 pounds
Full rear, medium-width hips
Small-to-medium waist
Medium-sized breasts
Average body type
Soft body tone
Blue eyes
Long, wavy hair,
(half say blond,
half say brown)
Smooth,
tanned skin

TRACING BODIES THROUGH TIME

Various reasons are given for why people originally began to wear clothes and/or adorn their bodies—including shame, protection, a desire to be different from the animals, and artistic expression. Regardless of the primary motivation, clothes have come to be used as one of the ways humankind overcomes feelings of inferiority and achieves a sense of superiority. Clothes win admiration and assure the wearer that he or she belongs to a certain ethnic, economic, or political group. What we wear enhances our self-importance and brings us pleasure, as well as admiration (or at least attention) from others. Clothes are not just functional or frivolous; they always mean something.

Most of what we know about a particular culture's body image has been revealed through the body shapes, clothing, and adornment disclosed in their art. In some of the earliest examples, the abundant figures of goddesses emphasized the female role in fertility and reflected the values of primitive society. Typical is the Venus of Willendorf, a prehistoric figure found in Austria. She is depicted with ample breasts, full abdomen, and underemphasized legs and arms.

Interestingly, the earliest adornments of the body were not so much practical as useful in conveying information about one's status, tribe, and availability. For hundreds of years, being fashionably dressed meant draping animal skins and primitively woven cloth over the body. Amazingly, Egyptian garments remained essentially the same from 3200 B.C. to 1500 B.C., with considerable interest in perfumes, make-up, and wigs. Nudity was associated with children and lower-class occupations.

By the time of the Greeks, tunics were worn by both sexes, women being distinguished by lighter and more delicate materials. Greek body image focused on being physically fit. Statues emphasized the male ideal and athletes were the only ones allowed to go nude in public. Beauty meant a proportionately balanced body with both aesthetic allure and strength.

The Greek *hetaerae*—a woman who today might be considered a high-class call girl—wore the finest clothes and make-up and the most elaborate hairstyles. Her evolution as a seductress outside the guidelines of respectability has contributed to the later ambivalence over the use of clothes and make-up for sexual attraction. By contrast, early Christian women were instructed to distinguish themselves by using clothes to "hide their shame" and to proclaim modesty and purity. Tertullian cautioned women, "You are the Devil's gateway... therefore, conceal your body."

The Romans focused more on facial appeal and greatly admired thinness. Since they also frequently enjoyed lavish banquets in which overindulgence was the rule, they alternated between cycles of bingeing and purging as a way to avoid obesity.

With a few exceptions, it wasn't until the Middle Ages that the chief emphasis in clothing and adornment was to reflect the difference between men and women. A major shift occurred in the fourteenth century. Since that time, female clothes have highlighted her sexual appeal. Male garments have been designed to enable him to do his perceived job of protecting and caring for women.

The Crusades influenced this new interest in clothes with the opposite sex in mind by making available new fabrics and handwork. The reproductive figure was idealized, with mother and child as a common theme of paintings. Being fat was considered erotic and fashionable. For the first time, the main garment was not loose, but rather cut to reveal a woman's figure and to emphasize whatever was considered most appealing at the moment. Low-cut necklines were adopted by most women, some displaying the entire breast. The style was a far cry from the church's original proclamation of modesty!

By the 1800s the emphasis was on waists and busts, with the lower body concealed by large skirts. Corsets came into fashion and were considered medical necessities for the "weaker" sex. Indeed, the steel or whalebone canvas cage left women with atrophied muscles and without the ability to take a deep breath. Over the corset, the Victorian lady wore several layers of shifts and chemises, several petticoats, a hoop skirt or crinoline, and a dress that might contain twenty yards of heavy material. A "lady"—not unlike her modern-day counterpart in tight skirt and spike heels—was most valued when she looked like a luxury.

Under the influence of the Puritan ethic, the United States advanced two versions of womanhood. Although both had corseted waists, one was delicate and frail, the other heavy and sexy. The delicate beauty was assumed to have high moral values and social status. The robust version, associated with actresses and prostitutes, was bustier, hippier, heavy-legged, and naturally from the lower class. Briefly during the 1880s, "big" became better and bottoms were broadened by bustles and padding.

Within a few years, the Gibson Girl became the ideal, her slender body and tallness accentuated by hair piled high. She was proper and graceful but not as delicate. Her bust and hips were large. She was the first to show a leg, since she participated in biking and swimming. During World War I, the flapper celebrated complete freedom from the corsets, bustles, and other paraphernalia that had previously been used to emphasize a woman's shape. She was a woman with a little boy's body. Brassieres were originally invented to help her diminish her bustline. For the first time in fashion history, the knee was exposed.

A more feminine look returned during the depression. Hemlines fell and the bust was back. By the forties, Betty Grable brought the leg into competition with the breast as the symbol of female eroticism. The fifties had its share of bosomy movie stars with the rise of Marilyn Monroe and Jane Russell. A second type of quieter beauty was popularized by Grace Kelly and Audrey Hepburn. The age-old question of whether you could be a lady and sexy at the same time was played out again, just as it had been since the days of the Greeks.

Emphasis on overpopulation during the sixties made the fertile earth mother image passé. In addition, the bikini and an anorexic thin model by the name of Twiggy began the current preoccupation with thinness. This ideal has been modified only slightly by the more muscular, healthy ideal personified by Jane Fonda and numerous other fitness gurus. Tracing the vital statistics of Miss America and famous fashion models, the idealized woman's body has consistently become taller and thinner.

RAPUNZEL AND COMPANY

From early times, hair has been a significant body image statement. Traditionally, long hair has been an attribute of femininity and sexuality. Married women have aroused their husbands in the privacy of the bedroom by loosening the long, full hair they kept pinned up during the day. Cutting the hair has always been associated with a drastic change of image, such as becoming a widow, losing a war, losing a love, or separating from the world for spiritual reasons. It frequently symbolized a rejection of sexual readiness.

The Bible provides some interesting sociological statements about the meaning of long hair or cutting the hair. For example, Esau the hunter was known for his extreme hairiness and Samson's uncut hair was the source of his superhuman strength. In contrast, Nazirites rejoining society shaved their hair. Or New Testament women covered their hair as a symbol of their submission to their husband's authority.[29]

Although there is no basis in fact that hair color determines personality, this has not stopped such conventional wisdom from developing. Such beliefs then tend to reinforce, by virtue of expectation, the stereotype in a person's life.

Blondes are supposed to have more fun and be preferred by men, although they are not supposed to be smart. Brunettes are emotional; redheads fiery and passionate.

Both Roman and Renaissance ladies bleached, dyed, and crimped their hair. No fairy tale princess could make it without her flaxen locks. Hair length for men has been a greater statement than hair color, although very light blond or red-gold shades are detrimental for men because they are closely associated with children and suggest immaturity and impulsiveness.

STRICTLY CLASS

Money provides the opportunity to buy the prevailing standard of beauty and body image. Historically, higher status was associated with more and more layers of clothing, which effectively prevented a person from doing any practical work! A pale complexion indicated wealth in Egypt, China, and Europe for it implied there was no need to be out in the sun. Powders were developed to further enhance the pale look. Even King Solomon's bride lamented as she compared herself to the ladies of the court. "Do not stare at me because I am dark, because I am darkened by the sun" (Sg 1:6). These days, only the rich can afford the vacation spots to keep a year-round tan while everyone else is working!

Today, women who are rich are more likely to be thin than those who are poor. Since the wealthy are emulated, they, along with the media, have contributed to acceptance of an anorexic standard as normal. Wealthy males, however, can sometimes be conspicuous by their bulk, thereby providing evidence that they have dined well and often and present imposing male power.[30] With increasing health consciousness, overweight is becoming increasingly associated with overindulgence.

Currently, the wealthy announce they are *somebody* by having so many clothes that repetition becomes unnecessary.

They wear a "costume" for each activity, the right shoes for racquetball, for instance, and another pair for running. Their outfits will most likely be of more costly natural fiber and the label will be on the outside. However, when something becomes accessible to the masses, it tends to quickly lose its appeal for the elite.

OUR KIDS DON'T ESCAPE

Unfortunately, children grow up facing the same stereotypes and pressures. Whereas adults concern themselves with the fact that Mrs. Roden has not lost her baby fat after the baby, and Mr. Kenner insists on polyester and looks like a hold-out from the fifties, children are more direct. Terms like "Fatso," "Metal Face," "Crater Face," and "Kansas Plains" are more their style.

Before long a child learns to value people according to their looks. Six-year-olds poke fun at peers who don't fit the prevailing standards of beauty. Even fathers have been shown to demonstrate more animosity toward their less attractive offspring and to give more attention to the cute infant.[31] At home, school, or out in society, homely children are blamed, punished, and mistreated more frequently. Some teachers will react differently to students depending on their looks.[32]

The chubby child endures the most negative stereotypes. Kindergarten children who are fat or thin are often not selected as popular or desirable buddies on tests designed to measure popularity. From middle childhood through early adolescence, how a child looks affects the likelihood of how close others get to him or her. These social interactions are not temporary annoyances. Body image, and consequently, feelings about interpersonal attractiveness and self-esteem, remain consistently more negative for fat children when tested at five, fifteen, and twenty years of age than for their average-weight peers.[33]

Dr. James Dobson, a leading authority on the family, writes

in his *Focus on the Family Magazine* about how many children's tales reinforce the stereotype that beautiful is good and ugly is bad.[34] For example, the witch in *Snow White and the Seven Dwarfs* personifies the link of ugliness and evil, whereas, Snow White is lovely, noble, and pure. *The Ugly Duckling* promises that if a person hangs in there long enough, maturity will result in a beauty that puts everyone else to shame. In real life, however, ugly little people frequently become ugly big people, a fact which no amount of magical thinking can alter.

Rudolph and Dumbo are mistreated because of their particular physical quirks, a theme young children are very familiar with. Neither is accepted until they accomplish miraculous feats that save the day. That's a lot to live up to to gain acceptance! Finally, there is Cinderella who marries a prince, outmaneuvers her ugly stepsisters, and ends up wearing ermine because she is pretty and has little feet.

THE SPECIAL WORLD OF THE TEEN

As we have already noted, parents and others draw conclusions, harbor expectations, and seek consciously or unconsciously through their attitudes and values to affect what we are to become. A child naturally wants to adapt to or make sense of the demands of significant others. As critical as those early years are, however, the teen years are crucial in the acceptance of one's body. Consequently, the timing and the adjustment to a new body image has a major bearing on how an individual feels about himself or herself as an adolescent and often as an adult.

Teens almost universally measure their self-worth by their physical attributes. Adolescents in grades six through nine who were diagnosed as being moderately to severely depressed were found to have less satisfaction with their bodies overall, viewed their bodies as less attractive, and felt they were less competent.[35] We become irritated when Johnny hogs the bathroom and Cindy makes everyone wait while she slips into yet another outfit. Yet their self-image is at stake, determined by the impression they are about to make by their physical appearance. That extra care and time and even Mom and Dad's wrath seem a small price to pay. No wonder a zit can seem the end of the world!

Since teens are the center of their own universe, they assume they are the center of everyone else's too. If you thought three hundred pairs of eyes watched your every move, you too would feel awkward and uncomfortable. Consequently, teasing a teen about an imagined or real defect can be very damaging. Teens need extra reassurance that imperfections are not fatal flaws. As they mature, adolescents begin to use other criteria for judging their value. Parents can foster this process by giving praise for real accomplishments.[36]

But at the age of fifteen, every flaw is magnified. I remember going out of my way to never allow anyone to see my feet. I perceived them as bony and ugly, undoubtedly warehouse rejects when God gave them to me. Today I have trouble seeing what was wrong with them. Such natural self-consciousness is more acute because of the tremendous physiological turmoil and changes an adolescent is going through. My husband began his fifteenth year enraged at his mother for having born him so small. His first love had just rejected him for a senior who was a head taller! By the end of the year, much to his relief, he had grown ten inches.

The unattractive teenager typically has fewer good friendships with classmates and more negative experiences with their peers. Their teachers tend to judge them as less able and more poorly adjusted. Chances are they will actually score lower on a standardized adjustment test. Parents report more troubles with their unattractive youngsters and the kids perceive themselves as having more problems.[37] By contrast, being good-looking makes a difference in dating popularity. And since practice makes perfect, attractive young males become more socially skilled with the opposite sex.[38]

Whereas boys will also consider sports or academics, many girls focus solely on the body as the source of their self-image.[39] How powerfully this affects their decision-making is demonstrated by a study designed to see what type of promotional material might encourage girls to strive for physical fitness. The girls preferred material that showed a slim model, but refused to heed the message to exercise. They were so afraid and self-conscious about being unable to identify with the slim ideal that they rejected the fitness message and activities. If they couldn't start out looking like the model, they weren't going to risk not measuring up![40]

Significant correlations can be seen between the way a girl is maturing and her behavior.[41] Apparently, changes in cognitive functioning make girls even more self-conscious than boys and thus intensifies their problems. The timing and significance given to breast development by girls and their peers can be very significant. When developing breasts signify change and adult status, a girl is likely to have more positive peer relationships, with better adjustment in general and a healthy body image.[42]

Kids naturally compare themselves to other kids to determine if they are normal. Therefore, their environment can make a difference in adjustment. If an early developing girl is in a kindergarten through sixth grade school, she will likely be more comfortable than if she were in a kindergarten through eighth grade setting. Older boys probably will put pressure on her for more adult behavior.[43] In the world of the dancer, the small delicate look is prized. Girls who are seriously involved with ballet have been found to be less likely to date and to view breast development as negative.[44]

No teen is insensitive to societal standards. Like their older sisters, young teenage girls have accepted thinness as the ideal. Since early maturers are often measurably and observably heavier and less lean than middle and late bloomers, they tend to be less satisfied with their bodies. Those who mature in the middle do fine unless their major pubertal changes are occurring in conjunction with entering junior high.[45] The unhappiest adolescents are those whose bodies don't fit the cultural mold of thinness and whose metamorphosis occurs simultaneously with changing schools, parental divorce, or other environmental upheavals.

THE DOWN SIDE FOR BEAUTIFUL PEOPLE

Barbara was one of those "drop-dead" beauties. From the time she cut her first tooth she was literally stopping traffic whenever she was taken in public. Life progressed smoothly until she reached dating age. Although most of her peers liked her, Barbara was the perennial wallflower at every dance and was rarely asked out on a date. Needless to say, she was confused. Even though she went out of her way to be friendly and nice, she and the "ugly" girls shared the same fate.

In college Barbara took an experiential psychology class. One of the exercises required the class members to share how they felt about one another. Barbara was amazed to discover that although the men universally found her attractive and appealing, most saw her as an untouchable princess to be admired from afar. Because she seemed so far beyond them, they would never ask her out. Rejection by someone so pretty was simply not worth the risk to their ego! They would instead date the more ordinary looking girl whose possible rejection would not be so painful.

The most hurtful revelation, however, was the evaluation from the women in the class. Barbara had never had a harsh word with any of them and they had cooperated on a number of projects. Yet their feelings toward her bordered on hate. Barbara was a rival with whom they could not compete and their emotions were controlled but intense.

Barbara's experience is not unique. Being liked by an attractive woman is more satisfying and brings inordinate pleasure to a man, but her rejection produces immense pain.[46] As long as the woman's actions and words appear positive, he likes her a lot. When he perceives she is losing interest in him, he responds with annoyance, aggression, and even hatred—much like he might react toward a woman he considered ugly.

Women have been taught that other women are their rivals, out to steal their man and not to be trusted. A real beauty is even more of a threat, for she is perceived as being able to have anyone she wants. Someone once said, "Being beautiful is like carrying a load of dynamite." An explosion can occur if the attractive person is insensitive to the effect he or she has on others. The more attractive, the more dynamite and the more extreme the potential reaction. People may want to please someone who is beautiful, but odds are also greater that they will be hated or disliked.

When making a presentation, an attractive woman who openly says she wants to influence her audience will be perceived positively. Such honesty by a male makes him immediately suspect.[47] It is not just an overactive imagination that makes a pretty woman appear to play dumb or at least less certain. By doing so she will have the greatest influence on men. Although women are swayed by the authoritative female, sadly, many men are more persuaded by and show a preference for those that appear to have less conviction.[48]

Barbara discovered that her beauty worked against her when she applied for her first job as a stock broker. Once she landed a job, her evaluations were often biased. Attractive women in traditionally male jobs must overcome the prejudice that they can't do the work like a man would. A pretty woman may rouse unwanted sexual advances, comments, and inferences. In a highly publicized case, a female neurosurgeon recently quit her position at Stanford Medical Center after years of sexual harassment. She put up with it, she stated, because as one of the few women in her field she felt pressured to fit in.

Beautiful women are also accused of getting ahead because of luck or sexual behavior. One man complained that he hated working with a beautiful woman because it made him feel like an inadequate adolescent back at his high school prom! "The cheerleader goddess appears and there is this jarring juxtaposition of feeling competent professionally and inadequate socially."

A female personnel director reports, "Men don't take a gorgeous woman seriously. They can't get their minds off her looks.... I will tell you that if you look like Christie Brinkley, you can forget becoming the CEO of a company that you do not own."[49] A beautiful professor explains her decision to gain thirty pounds: "In academia it is detrimental to be particularly attractive because you're not taken seriously. Also, people can be jealous, and it can take away from a woman's authority. Academics is a nerdy profession and people do not spend a lot of time cultivating their appearance."

Other areas of discrimination cut across both sexes. Good-looking people are viewed in a more sexist way: females as more feminine, males as more masculine. Conventional wisdom proclaims that, "What is beautiful is self-centered." While society attributes all kinds of wonderful traits to the attractive, it turns around and accuses them of believing what everyone else believes about them! They are charged with thinking they are superior: the handsome man who ignores you is stuck up, not shy; the appealing couple with the new baby and the three-year-old can't possibly be devoted parents; and, everyone knows the "hunk" or the "looker" can't be faithful.

When it comes to body image, extremes can be difficult. Life can be tough if a person doesn't fall into that magic middle ground that provides some relief from considerations of body image. In the end, the downside of being beautiful is far outweighed by the discrimination against the homely. Our habit of admiring the beautiful in the long run is less advantageous to them than it is harmful to the unattractive.

IS BEAUTY IN THE EYE OF THE BEHOLDER?

In case you think the beauty bias is a Western phenomenon, it's not. All cultures favor the beautiful even though their standards may vary. Beauty is not met by one particular criterion or easily defined to the satisfaction of all, but what a large segment of any population says it is. Beauty usually includes regular features that don't vary much from the average. Universally appealing traits include firm breasts, roundness of hips, fleshiness versus flabbiness, symmetry, and smooth skin. As the world grows smaller and the media reaches previously isolated places, we can expect the standards for what is beautiful to become more uniform.

We find it tempting to dismiss such considerations of body image and beauty as entertaining but insignificant. That would be a mistake. The way we have organized and integrated the experiences of our body influences each of us profoundly—personally and professionally. We have no choice but to conclude that the effects on a person of being physically attractive or unattractive are certainly *not* superficial.

SELF-AWARENESS QUIZ I
How Body Conscious Are You?

The following questions will help to make you aware of the stereotypes and prejudices you may hold. Stereotypical thinking is not only detrimental for others but also hurts us when we judge ourselves by the same biased criteria. If you answer yes to more than ten of the following questions, you may need to rethink the influence body image has on your life... and ultimately your happiness.

1. Do you buy or subscribe to more than one fashion or self-improvement magazine?

       yes_____   no_____

2. Do you have several "looks" or wardrobes in your closet that represent different phases you have gone through in finding your image?

yes_____   no_____

3. Are you unhappy with your weight?

yes_____   no_____

4. Do you belong to a gym because you enjoy it?

yes_____   no_____

5. Do you feel superior to others because your body is closer to the societal ideal than most?

yes_____   no_____

6. Do you feel inferior to others because your body does not match the societal ideal?

yes_____   no_____

7. Have your looks ever stopped you from applying for a job, striving for a new position, or introducing yourself to someone?

yes_____   no_____

8. Do you wear make-up, clothes, or use things or money to distract from the fact you don't feel pretty or handsome?

yes_____   no_____

9. Do you believe your success has been hampered by your looks?

yes_____   no_____

10. Do you feel more comfortable around people with a certain body type?

yes_____   no_____

11. Do you feel depressed by the models in advertisements?

yes_____   no_____

12. Do you secretly resent beautiful people?

      yes_____   no_____

13. When someone compliments you on your appearance are you comfortable?

      yes_____   no_____

14. Do you look in a mirror more than five times a day?

      yes_____   no_____

15. Do you weigh yourself more than once a week?

      yes_____   no_____

16. Do you feel competitive with most people?

      yes_____   no_____

17. If you make a fashion mistake are you unreasonably embarrassed?

      yes_____   no_____

18a. If you are a man, do a woman's looks influence how you work with her?

      yes_____   no_____

18b. If you are a woman, do you judge how another woman looks more harshly than how a man looks?

      yes_____   no_____

19. Do you avoid activities that use the body such as dance, exercise, and sports?

      yes_____   no_____

20. Do you dislike having your body touched?

      yes_____   no_____

3

The Illusive Ideal

S O MANY STUDIES SUGGEST that beautiful people
derive tremendous advantages that we would
expect them to be holding the most positions of power, raising beautiful children, and enjoying relationships with other
beautiful people. After all, the media frequently portrays just
such a scenario. But real life demonstrates that factors other
than appearance are also at work. Neither beauty nor home-
liness guarantees a rosy future or how a person will feel about
his or her body.

Consider Frank Peretti, whose novels, *This Present Darkness*
and *Piercing the Darkness* have sold over two million copies.
His storytelling ability and vivid imagination has much to do
with the fact that this man was born with a tumor growing in
his jaw and tongue.

Even though several operations eventually corrected the
problem, Peretti learned to talk with his tongue outside his
mouth. He remembers his tongue as being big and ugly and
full of scabs. Feeling like a monster with his disfigurement
and speech impediment, Peretti began entertaining other
kids with mesmerizing tales of monsters. He recalls, "They
were ugly and so was I. I envied the fact that they were strong
and people were scared of them."[1] At the age of twelve he was

trained to speak with his tongue in his mouth and life became decidedly better. But Peretti's course as a storyteller had already been set.

Mark is another example of a childhood anomaly determining a direction for life. He was born with gastroesophageal reflux. As his food digested, it moved back up into his esophagus, causing burning and discomfort. The only relief came from eating. Mark loved to eat because it provided comfort. As he grew, adults loved the fact that he relished eating what they had prepared. Other kids took advantage of his willingness to accommodate anyone on the playground who needed to return home with an empty lunch box!

Because Mark was heavy *and* big as a youngster, people noticed and often commented on his size. Overeating finally left Mark tilting the scales at over three hundred fifty pounds. Since few girls were interested in dating him, he became "the shoulder to cry on," "the peer counselor" for one's woes. It is not surprising that at age twenty-six, Mark is pursuing a line of work that has provided the only satisfactory relationships he has enjoyed: providing help and counsel as a psychologist.

For most people, the outside world's reaction is not as crucial as what happens within our own family in influencing our future development, adjustment, and happiness. Young children often have little more than their parents and siblings to give them the first and most lasting impressions of how they measure up as a person.

My friend Katy began life hidden from public view because her mother considered her ugly. Her acquired sense of self-rejection and disgust was reinforced by an incestuous father. As a child she began to split off from the "ugly, disgusting Katy" into alternatives of herself better able to deal with various demands of her life. Only much later as an adult and a mother herself was she finally able to embrace and live with the beautiful Katy God had created. Today she wears a tee shirt that proclaims, "It is never too late to have a happy childhood."

Trish was battered and abused emotionally by a schizophrenic mother and a cruel father. He announced to her at thirteen that she would be a whore. Smart enough to check out reality, Trish would go out for a walk to see if she could make a person smile. "I succeeded, I had power and counted, if I could do that." Out of fear of her father's prophecy, for years she allowed no one to get close to her physically.

Eventually Trish married. Now in her late forties, she has raised six children while unrelentingly upgrading her education. Her father's proclamation that she would have to use her body to succeed since she lacked the necessary brain power drove her to become an expert. Besides being a college-educated nurse and an obstetric-gynecological nurse practitioner, Trish has two doctorates, one just completed at UCLA.

Sylvester Stallone is one of the world's highest paid movie stars. Few in the world would not recognize his characters Rocky and Rambo. Born in a charity ward in New York City, Stallone's difficult delivery left him paralyzed on the lower left side of his face. The result was a lopsided mouth and slurred speech. The future Rambo was born with a unique ability to look menacing because of the set-in snarl.

Stallone maintains that he started smiling at forty-two years of age. Perhaps the fact that smiling was difficult helps explain why kids hated him and frequently picked on him. Or maybe it had to do with his scrawny body and crooked mouth. A Steve Reeves movie, *Hercules*, seemed to provide a way out for a kid who had been told by his abusive father that his "brain was dormant." Even his teachers said he was dumb, so Stallone decided he had better develop his body. He says, "I was very heavy into body building. It came from deep-rooted insecurity. You kind of create a muscular shell to protect that soft inside. You try to build yourself into the image that you think people will respect, and it tends to get a little extreme. It's like playing God, rebuilding your body in your own image."[2]

THE UGLY DUCKLING OF THE BIBLE

Stallone's choice to gain power and respect by developing his body is in line with the options open to men. Producing a male heir was the pathway open to Leah (see Gn 29:9-35). Born during the days of the patriarchs, her options were few. Leah could easily be called the ugly duckling of the Bible, although she never grew to be a beautiful swan. Real life is much more complex.

Leah certainly suffered as a result of not meeting the standards of beauty of her time. To make matters worse, she lived in the same house with a sister who was a bonafide "ten." In true soap opera fashion, Leah became caught up in a love triangle involving her husband and sister. Leah's husband was Jacob, the ancient patriarch who was infamous for stealing his brother Esau's blessing from their father, Isaac. In truth, Jacob never wanted to marry Leah. The very first time he laid eyes on her younger sister, Rachael, he fell head over heels in love with her. Why? Because she was a spiritual giant? No! Because she was a knockout.

When the time came for Rachael and Jacob to marry, the girls' father cunningly took advantage of veils, darkness, and too much wine. Later claiming an obligation to marry off his older daughter first, he substituted Leah on his wedding night. Imagine how you would feel if your own father considered you so ugly and undesirable that the only way he could get rid of you was to trick someone into marrying you! Jacob was livid. He had no love for Leah.

Leah's name means "wild cow," while Rachael's name stands for "Ewe," the herdsman's prized possession. Leah also is described as having weak eyes. Poor vision may explain why the younger daughter Rachael was out tending the sheep instead of the eldest. Or perhaps she had a common eye disease of the time that caused welts and open sores around the eyes. Rachael is described as beautiful in form and face. Leah was the opposite: ugly, no figure, funny eyes, and maybe a lousy complexion.

We are told that the Lord saw that Leah was unloved and opened her womb. The names of her children may tell us the rest of the story. Her firstborn, Reuben, means "to see or perceive." Leah sought to be seen, if only through her son, the greatest gift a Hebrew woman could give her husband. Simeon stands for "having heard or hearing." Leah was an ignored person; through Simeon she asked to be heard. Levi means "to bind together, attach to." His birth said to Jacob, "Please attach to me, instead of using me."

But bearing three sons had still not won Jacob's heart. Leah's focus shifted. She named her fourth son Judah, which means "to celebrate in worship." She gave up trying to win her husband's attention and turned to God for the significance and security she needed. Leah discovered someone *was* paying attention and listening to her, indeed holding an unwavering commitment to her.

God chose an unattractive, rejected soul, an "ugly duckling" to establish the house of Judah—the lineage from which Jesus would come. Given the choice, most men would likely have picked Rachael as well. She appeared to have more to offer than Leah. But as the Apostle Paul explains, God has composed the body—that is, the church—giving more abundant honor to that member which is lacking (1 Cor 12:14-26). God put this same principal into practice thousands of years earlier with Leah.

Perhaps today Leah would not have looked to God for a solution to her pain. She might have turned instead to some aspect of the "positive thinking" movement, joined a gym, visited a plastic surgeon, or maybe even read *Cosmopolitan* magazine! It's editor, Helen Gurley Brown, would suggest a different approach for Leah. "At the table, be a little geisha-like... butter his roll, put the sugar alongside his coffee," would be a typical bit of advice from its pages.[3]

Cosmopolitan, Ms. Brown says, is dedicated to young women who are not naturally blessed with beauty, status, and wealth. Her advice to the Leahs of the world is to work very hard, have hope, and they too will have power. The promise is of upward mobility. "One thing I do quite well," she states, "is deal with reality."[4] Apparently a lot of people agree with Brown's choice of handling an imperfect body image. Her magazine is one of the five largest selling magazines in the United States.

OVERCOMING THE IMPOSSIBLE

Betty Baxter grew up knowing that there was nothing she nor anyone else could do to enable her to meet even the most minimal standards of competence and beauty.[5] Her own sister couldn't bear to visit her room. Betty's pain-wracked little body was curled up and deformed, her arms paralyzed, her fingers barely moveable. The outside form merely reflected the turmoil internally, where organs were misplaced and an enlarged heart made it difficult to breathe.

Unable to eat regular food, Betty was kept alive with liquids and intravenous feeding. Memories of her childhood do not include one single day of good health. Her parents desperately took her from one clinic to the next, seeking healing for a child who was so deformed that they could not put clothes or shoes on her. The prognosis was always the same: there was no hope.

Betty's parents were devoted to their faith. They sought to comfort their dying daughter by reading the Bible to her. Betty loved the passages which illustrated that although appearance and perfect health might be desirable for serving humankind, they weren't necessary to be of value to God.

The comfort Betty found as she reread Scripture prompted her to become a Christian when she was nine years old. Immediately, the bitterness she felt over her contorted body was gone, but ironically, her condition worsened. She identified with the woman in Luke 13:11-12 who had been crippled for eighteen years: "She was bent over and could not straighten up at all. When Jesus saw her, he called her forward and said to her, 'Woman, you are set free from your infirmity.'"

How Betty longed to be set free. When she stood, her body was so crooked and bent that her head was by her knees. Sometimes she would be propped in a large armchair. Her parents would have to lounge on the floor to look into her face. Despite their church's teaching that the gift of healing was not for modern times, her mother clung to the promise that Jesus was the same yesterday, today, and tomorrow. He had healed in the past and he could heal her daughter today. Betty begged for recovery, but like many disabled persons she also longed for heaven where she knew she would be free of pain, no longer a prisoner of her twisted body.

Betty hated being isolated, but visitors were banned because they created too much stress on her frail heart. Her sanity was preserved by the sense that she was not alone. Betty knew that Jesus was with her. At fifteen she lapsed into a coma from which recovery was not deemed possible. Near death, she experienced a vision in which she again begged Jesus to take her to heaven. This time, she received a promise of healing.

Four months later, Betty regained consciousness, anticipating her recovery. Both she and her mother had been independently made aware of a date and time. Her mother's faith was so great that she bought a dress and shoes for the daughter who had never owned either.

The day and time arrived. Relatives and friends appeared for what they were convinced would be a humiliating disappointment. Betty was brought into the living room and her mother began to pray. Miraculously, within minutes, the promise of healing was realized. Accompanied by an audible cracking of bones and the sense of internal changes that brought immediate relief to her labored breathing, Betty stood up straight and strong.

Two weeks later, Betty began her life's work: traveling and telling her story as a missionary evangelist. She married, had children and grandchildren, and has tirelessly maintained a schedule that could only be kept by the most fit!

THE DICTATES OF BEAUTY

Society urges us to try harder to meet the prevailing standards of beauty or forever live with our insecurities. Desperately seeking acceptance under such pressure is not a healthy way to live. Frank Peretti, Katy, Mark, and Trish found ways—some healthy, some not so sound—to compensate for their sense of not measuring up. Sylvester Stallone and Leah sought acceptance through exaggeration of traits considered admirable for their sex and in their frame of reference. Betty turned to a supernatural source.

How are we supposed to live in a world in which the evaluation of our worth appears so dependent on our physical attributes? Each of these overcomers followed some of the following principles:

- Do not accept things as they are.
- Be creative in finding solutions.
- Reframe the problem to work for you.
- Seek excellence in some area of your life.
- Persevere!

Anyone who rises above such difficult life circumstances deserves great admiration. But the question must still be asked: what is our source of validation to be? What if God's answer to a new nose is no? Are we, like Stallone, to remake our body into our own image? If life gives us lemons in the form of an endomorphic shape, are we to make lemonade by distracting people's attention to our accomplishments or jokes or cooperative nature?

In fact, even natural beauty doesn't count unless we believe it. Being attractive does not always insure that an individual will have a healthy body image. To most of us, movie star Sally Field has a lot going for her. She is attractive, talented, and wealthy. In a recent poll, Sally Field was chosen the woman American men would most like to be married to. That is quite an affirmation!

In reference to her own husband, however, Field herself ponders, "Just supposing he was not ready to settle down, would he still be attracted to me? These are the questions in the wee small hours that short brunette women who are married to people who dated tall blondes ask themselves."[6] Even Sally Field sees herself as somehow lacking because she is not tall, thin, and blonde. Her high school girlfriends had told her she was too short and dark to make it in Hollywood. Such is the power of a lingering body image!

Sally Field responded upon accepting the Oscar for her performance in *Norma Rae*, "You *like* me, you *really* like me!" Will she feel *unliked* at the next nomination when she doesn't win? Will the young reader of *Cosmopolitan* who has religiously followed Helen Gurley Brown's formula for success—exercising, plastic surgery, super-seductress behaviors, attention to job achievements—actually find it?

Betty's and Leah's solution to problems with body image was found by looking to God instead of the standard advice. Are they special cases, or is there an important truth to be gleaned from their experience? Clearly, the quality of people's lives is not always dictated by beauty or lack thereof. Accepting the prevailing standard is not necessarily essential, enriching, or permanent.

Those who succeed despite perceived or real traits that are considered undesirable don't dwell on idealized images of themselves. To do so would only be immobilizing and depressing. Instead, such people view themselves *realistically*. They see the negative but it does not blind them to the good they possess. Those with a healthy self-image are able to look beyond childhood experiences, expectations of parents, traumas, and the prevailing standard of what is valuable and acceptable. They find neglected or forgotten pleasures.

Is an image of a perfect self a stumbling block that keeps *you* from reclaiming the total aspect of who you are? Has a discrepancy between your *ideal* self and your *real* self pushed you into a frenetic whirl of self-improvement programs? Is it possible that over the long run those activities have resulted in your feeling even *less* capable? Are you positive the prescription you are taking is the correct one for the pain you feel?

PERSONAL HISTORY PART I

Who and What Has Influenced You?

There are no right or wrong answers for these questions designed to help you think about the influences in your own life. Were they positive? Did they leave you with good feelings about your body? Is there a pattern? Are you still influenced by them?

1. What message did your mother give you about your attractiveness and/or physical ability, or lack of it?

2. What message did your father give you about your attractiveness and/or physical ability, or lack of it? (If you were raised by someone else, consider their message and what you were told about your birth parents' reaction to you.)

3. Do you feel better or worse about your body than you did five years ago?

4. Were your looks ever the subject of your classmates' ridicule or humor?

5. Did you ever have a nickname that related to some aspect of your body?

6. When did you first become aware of the pressure to look a certain way?

7. Do you have a sense of humor about your appearance?

8. What traits do you possess that are valuable to you which you may have overlooked or neglected?

9. Being realistic means acknowledging the bad and good. Make a list that includes an equal number of both traits that are true for you.

Part Two

Mirror, Mirror
on the Wall

Sex and beauty are inseparable, like life and consciousness.
David Herbert Lawrence, 1885–1930

Beauty is in the eye of the beholder.
Margaret Worlfe Hungerford, 1855–1897

Beauty's but skin deep.   **John Davis of Hereford, 1565–1618**

Beauty in things exists in the mind which contemplates them.
David Hume, 1711–1776

There are women who are not beautiful but only look that way.
Karl Kraus, 1874–1936

4

Sex Appeal

*T*HE FEEDBACK WE RECEIVE and experiences we have with others directly influence how we evaluate our masculinity or femininity. Some people relish and enjoy who they are as a man or as a woman. But how well we *perform* in that role with someone of the other sex is—rightly or wrongly—what most affects our conclusions.

Consequently, we tend to put tremendous energy into attracting the opposite sex. This should come as no surprise, since men and women were created to desire relationship with one another. These efforts to be attractive further serve to define who we are as a male or female. The media have become an influential reference point for judging how well we are doing. Indeed, media images provide the unspoken standard by which we often judge our own and other's sexuality. The messages are simple and unambiguous:

- You can buy sex appeal.
- A great body will result in great sex and happiness.
- Sex is for the young and beautiful.
- Sex is for the healthy.
- You can create a sexy body if you work hard enough.

YOU CAN BUY SEX APPEAL

The cover of a recent issue of *Cosmopolitan* entices its young audience with titles such as these: "How to Have All the Dates You Can Handle" and "Are You a Sexual Sleeping Beauty? Turn to Page 140 for Your Wake-up Call." The article regarding more dates begins with a little Cosmo advice. Keep up the "self-maintenance." You wouldn't want "Mr. Romance" to find you flabby with dull hair. The experienced male authority concludes the same article with this advice: "Don't do it on the first date." Why? "We just don't want them [women] to take away the illusion of control. Going to bed with a girl on the first date can get scary. What's left for the third date... marriage?"[1] "Your Wake-up Call" simply states that sex gets better with practice, a variety of partners, and as a woman becomes more comfortable with her own body.

Such is the conventional wisdom and teaching about sex today. Should we be surprised? I think not. The media rarely offers a sane, lucid, and responsible voice which places sex in a purposeful context. Sex is reduced to sex for its own sake— ignoring the undeniable fact that how we view our bodies as sexual men or women profoundly affects our ability to function in life, our happiness, and ultimately the health of our families.

Powerful media messages presented in television, music, movies, and print motivate us to buy products that will preserve our youth and sex appeal. "Daily support against the effects of aging," advertises Niosome, a creme which promises youthful looking skin. Hair color is painted as crucial to a beautiful you: "Who knows, maybe you've always been beautiful, you just needed a little shove. Nice 'n' Easy color. You, only better. It's from Clairol."

Models, some as young as eleven, are seductively strewn across the pages. They set a standard of beauty that is to be emulated, while ignoring the impact of hormones, bearing children, and the passage of time on adult bodies. Robin

Jones, director of scouting for Elite, one of the world's top modeling agencies, reports, "If they haven't gotten started by age twenty, you got to bury them."

The link of youthfulness, fine-tuned bodies, and sexuality is sometimes even more blatant in perfume ads. For example, Obsession and Eternity, Calvin Klein's top-selling scents, are advertised through a powerful sexual image of a nude man carrying a limp, nude woman over his shoulders. Another version suggests sexual attraction to children; one glamorizes obsessive love. Ambivalence about sexuality is also reflected at the cosmetic counter. In the 1950s Ponds offered an Angel Face line of products. Today we hear of Red Door, Tabu, and Fire & Ice. There is Joy, Saint, and Passion. And for those who are ready to skip the titillation and embrace the promise of raw sexuality: Opium, Poison, and Evil.

Make-up has often been criticized for its deceptive element. Our English word *pretty* is derived from an Old English adjective meaning *tricky*. Heavy cosmetic use in our Western culture has always been associated with the seductive temptress. Even today too heavy a hand is considered unrefined. Advertisers choose their vocabulary carefully. Cover Girl's Perfecting Make-up promises the illusion of perfection, while Ultima II's The Nakeds insinuates that the illusion created is not an illusion!

Being attractive is big business because it holds out the promise of a sexual relationship. The fantasy that looking good is the key to love, fulfillment, happiness, and thus meaning in our lives, keeps cash registers ringing.

A GREAT BODY WILL RESULT IN GREAT SEX AND HAPPINESS

Why we fall in love with one particular person and not another is often a mystery. Men and women approach love and lovemaking with different agendas. When I first dated my husband, I was pleased that he was nice looking and had a swimmer's body. But it was equally important to me that he was from a wonderful, loving family and that he wanted to be a physician. My eligibility list included descriptors such as "bright" and "capable of providing a stable home." Sexual attraction was on the list, but by no means at the top.

Imagine my disappointment when I discovered that my husband's list contained these two items: great legs and potential sex partner. Didn't he see how bright I was? Wasn't he impressed with my compassion and sensitivity? My loyalty? My composure? No, like the vast majority of males, it was the physical that made an impact—at least in the beginning.

Attacking men for their proclivity for a woman's body seems easy and justifiable. No one wishes to be seen as one-dimensional. But being attracted to the female form is part of the distinctness of being male.

Almost every culture has some lore or myth to explain the magnetism that so obviously attracts men and women. Plato talked of a "he/she" sphere with four arms, legs, and two heads that rebelled against Zeus, its maker. In anger, he cut the sphere in half. Each half seeks the other to be complete.

In Christianity, when Adam was first introduced to Eve, he responded with what would have been the modern day equivalent to, "WOW!" Adam's only disappointment in God's creation had been his failure to find anyone to love or be a partner uniquely fitted to him. Having been made in the image of God, men and women were to desire relationship with one another. Adam and Eve did, unabashed and unashamed in their innocence.

Along with Scripture, research[2] and common sense agree that the majority of men are highly attuned to the physical. "To men a man is but a mind. Who cares what face he carries or form he wears? But woman's body is the woman," observed a somewhat sexist Ambrose Bierce in the 1800s.

Men naturally notice faces and bodies, for the visual is what arouses a man. A woman who insists on lights out for lovemaking is eliminating much of what a male uses for erotic stimulation. Allowing a husband's eyes to roam over what he was designed to love is a passionate signal to him. A man wants sex; a woman wants to make love. He wants to share pleasure; she desires affection and commitment. His focus is on achieving a goal of physical passion and playful, lusty sex; her aim is to experience an emotional connection.

Must it always be this way? Will the twain ever meet? Yes and no. As marriage partners mature in a healthy and vital relationship, they will occasionally and unself-consciously switch roles. Will they ever look on their body and its purpose in exactly the same way? Probably not.

When men and women fail to understand the way the other sex perceives the body, conflict often ensues. Because men are often ready and eager for physical intimacy, they can easily interpret any provocative dress or behavior as a signal that the woman is inviting or at least prepared for more sexualized behavior. A man may find it difficult to believe that she might be merely saying, "I am a desirable woman" or, "I want you to admire me but not touch." Since visual presence is not usually their primary consideration, women frequently underestimate the impact their appearance has on men. Such muddled messages are at the heart of many date-rape and sexual assault situations.

At the height of the women's movement, men were put down for any conduct toward a woman that would not also be appropriate for a man. *Ms* magazine recommended that women quit wearing make-up or practicing any behavior that would encourage men to view them in a sexual way. Such overreaction resulted in a denial of the very characteristics that make women unique.

Worse, this mindset suggested that to be a worthwhile woman, you had to be more like a man. So strong was the bias against possible sexism that researchers who worked with demonstrable differences between the sexes found few professional journals would publish their work. I find it refreshing and perversely humorous to see the scientific community currently "rediscovering" the innate differences between men and women.

The concept that sex is no big deal has resulted not in sexual freedom, but rather *inhibited desire* or *avoidance of sex* altogether. Some people attempt to use sex to bolster self-esteem by sizing up their performance and that of their partners. Was the sexual encounter a good one? Was I good? How many? How long?

Lovemaking is not just a matter of going through the motions. It encompasses caring, gentleness, and trust. The suggestion that sex can be recreational without love takes a tremendous toll emotionally and spiritually. So does the idea that sex is simple. Most people innately understand that merely learning a new position is a simplistic response to such a complex issue.

SEX IS FOR THE YOUNG AND BEAUTIFUL

In my work as a sex therapist, I often see couples who have run into the buzzsaw of sexual folklore. If we believe the promises of the media, Shawn and Sharon should have been able to make madly passionate love the first time they tried. They were young, athletic, and attractive. Shawn was deeply in love with Sharon, but their lovemaking was always traumatic for him. They were virgins when they married and neither had read or been taught much about sex.

This couple expected that God would honor their decision to wait by giving them a great sex life. But Shawn had a body image problem and always felt less endowed than his peers. When things did not go smoothly, he assumed it was the fault of his own inadequacy. Shawn unwittingly became a spectator to their lovemaking, watching for any sign that Sharon was not enjoying his advances. By six months, he routinely lost his erection shortly after penetration.

Anyone who has ever played a sport is aware of the tremendous boost of having your own cheering squad, a little group of spectators who take your side and yell and hoot at your every move. The trouble with having a spectator when you are making love is that you have to simultaneously be the *player* and the *onlooker*. Your mind and body are split. Your body no longer registers the sensations that are coming in. And your mind, operating against all good spectating rules, becomes your worst fan.

Fortunately for Shawn and Sharon, their new pastor was sensitive and educated about sexuality. He was able to help them understand that God certainly honored their abstinence, but that their expectations had not been realistic. Sex, like anything else, requires *learning* and *practice*. Since two people are involved, *good communication* is essential as well. Most importantly, he addressed Shawn's belief that his penis was too small by reassuring him that all are approximately the same size when erect. Shawn also learned that the sensitive areas of his wife's body were external or only in the lower third of the vagina. He came to realize there was no objective basis for his sense of inadequacy.

People diminish their sexual responsiveness by constantly spectating, especially if they are distracted by some real or perceived body defect. One woman's internal spectator made it impossible for her to focus on incoming sensations of arousal by yelling, "He can't possibly love you! Your thighs are too fat." A common spectator message is, "You're so ugly, you don't deserve any pleasure or approval!"

Even the "Body Beautiful" or the "Stud" is not immune from the effects of spectating. The other extreme of focusing on how great you look or make love can equally diminish sensual input. The long-term result of being a spectator is functioning with little sense of pleasure or being unable to respond.

Linda's husband struggled with the reality that her weight gain made a difference to him. She was a wonderful wife and mother, but she hardly resembled the one-hundred-eighteen-pound beauty he had married. When Linda became pregnant for the third time, Jim created quite a stir in the physician's office by insisting on watching her initial weigh-in. They were both shocked to see the scales register two hundred sixty-five pounds. While Linda had struggled to cope with her weight by avoidance and lapsing into depression, Jim had lost all interest in having sex.

When Chuck's wife gained her weight at an average of five pounds per month, he continued sexual relations. Nonetheless, he experienced increasing conflict over his escalating use of fantasizing about other women to ensure his arousal.

Are women equally turned off when their spouse no longer looks like the high school track star? Although women appreciate a trim body, their sexual responsiveness is likely to be affected more by other aspects of the relationship. The fact that women do not usually put physical attractiveness at the top of their "perfect-mate list" explains why you see someone as beautiful as Sophia Loren married to the short, stout, and balding Carlo Ponti. Of course there are always exceptions. On the day I wrote this section, I received a letter from a woman who is so turned off by her husband's weight that she is fearful for their marriage.

Other factors inhibit healthy sexual expression besides spectating and obsessing about how our bodies don't meet the *Cosmo* standard. One example is perceiving the body or certain body parts as "dirty." Cindy faced this issue as she geared up for having her dreaded annual physical. She was grimly anticipating slipping back into her clothes and getting out of what felt like a torture chamber. Then the doctor announced that the pap smear was all that was left to be done. If it weren't for the fact that her mother had died of uterine cancer, Cindy would have gladly skipped this part. To make matters worse, her gynecologist believed in patient education. She wished he would just shut up and get on with it.

Suddenly her heart stopped. Had he really asked her to take hold of the mirror and look? Why was he so insistent? Thoroughly panicked, Cindy grabbed the mirror and launched it across the room. Silence. Next time she would go to a doctor who couldn't speak English!

Cindy's embarrassment and perception of her body as

dirty made the thought of looking at it or thinking of it positively impossible. Needless to say, her sexual relationship was
unrewarding. If a body's owner can't touch it with comfort,
certainly another person can't either. One of the first steps in
sexual counseling is to increase the individual's comfort level
with their own body. Sometimes this can be the biggest hur-
dle to overcome.

Small children can easily conclude that their genitals are
dirty when diapering and cleaning chores have been accompanied by negative words, sounds, and gestures, with no distinction having been made between the anal sphincter and
genitals. Others feel uncomfortable because genitals haven't
been discussed at all, assuming that things that aren't talked
about are bad. The vast majority of girls, for example, are
never told they have a clitoris, despite the fact that it plays an
essential role in a woman's sexual response.

Mrs. Crowell's trip to the doctor was to remind him again
not to tell her husband that she had breast implants. He had
never seen the scars because she insisted on keeping the
lights out when they made love. Her concern that her body
be "naturally perfect" extended to resisting a necessary Caesarian section when it became evident that her baby was in
jeopardy. Mrs. Crowell refused to consent even when two
doctors confirmed she needed the surgery to ensure the
health of her child. Her delay is indicative of how important
her body image was to her. When a healthy baby was finally
delivered by Caesarian, Mrs. Crowell sued the doctors because of the mental anguish of having to live with the scar.

For some, pregnancy itself can result in a body image that
can be an amorous turn-on. Many pregnant women received
a considerable boost in perceiving their bodies as beautiful
and sexy when Demi Moore appeared on the cover of *Vanity
Fair*—nude and eight months pregnant. Reaction to this
cover photo was intense, apparently split down the middle.
Moore's picture generated ninety-five different television
pieces with one hundred ten million viewers, sixty-four radio

shows, and more than fifteen hundred newspaper articles, according to the following month's *Vanity Fair.* Some comments were along this line: "This is a desecration. Like sex, pregnancy is a wonderful experience, but one which when observed by someone else becomes repulsive and pornographic." Others responded on the other extreme: "A new Eve. Perfect."

But Moore's motivation had as much to do with her non-pregnant body image as it did with her delight at being pregnant and the good esteem with which she views her expanded body. Her decision to appear in such a controversial and unprecedented layout has more to it than the obvious. As a child she was extremely skinny and had problems with a weak eye muscle that required surgery and caused her to have to occasionally wear a patch. She remembers herself as "pathetic." Moore reflected, "To grow to puberty and not have anybody pay attention to me meant my feelings were unimportant, nonexistent."[3] Perhaps her revealing photographs ensure her the attention she lacked as a child and reinforce the fact that her body now makes an impact.

The days are long gone of hiding pregnancy and referring to it by euphemisms such as "with child" and "that way." Even so, many people still have serious problems with the association of sex and motherhood. Some women experience a temporarily heightened focus on mothering after childbirth—especially if nursing. But as their body returns to a nonpregnant state, most are happy to re-embrace their body image as lover as well.

Some men view the body and its sexual desires as the site of evil, and conversely eulogize motherhood as saintly and "sexless." When you think about it, such joint conclusions require considerably convoluted reasoning! Men who take such attitudes to the extreme may suffer from the "Madonna/Whore" Syndrome—finding it difficult to passionately love their wives while having no problem with a mistress.

Singer Elvis Presley was known for the love and esteem

with which he revered his mother. He met his future wife, Priscilla, when she was only fourteen years old. Although Priscilla says they shared years of very erotic behavior, Elvis insisted intercourse be reserved for marriage. He had no such sexual hesitation with women who were not his potential marriage partner. Marital sexuality was normal and satisfying until Priscilla gave birth to their daughter, after which Elvis rarely approached his wife. During this time, he was linked with a number of women whose image lacked the innocence and purity he insisted upon in his wife.[4]

Some couples spend months or years focusing on pregnancy as the primary motivator and reason for sex. If they are unable to conceive, they may begin to feel there is no reason to make love "if the purpose of it can never be fulfilled." It is a faulty body image which keeps a person from feeling "like a man" or "like a real woman" because of the inability to conceive, thus undermining the emotional and physical relationship.

Despair over the inability to conceive prompts some people to spend inordinate amounts of money for modern technology that offers only slim chances of success. Besides wanting a child of their own, the desire to have completed one's destiny as a male or female can be an underlying drive. I believe this drive is also tied to a person's body image.

When different cultures offer women fewer outlets for accomplishment, the pressure to bear children is even more intense. Consider Hannah, a Hebrew woman whose story is told in the Old Testament. Her husband assured her that his love for her was better than if she had given him ten sons—quite an affirmation in a society where one's name and duty to God was carried on through the birth of sons.

But Hannah could not be consoled. In desperation she wept and petitioned the Lord. She was so thin from not eating, weary looking, and so frantic, that the priest thought she was drunk. Fortunately for Hannah, her prayers were heard and she gave birth to the most famous priest of Israel,

Samuel. When she received this promise through the priest, she ate and "her face was no longer downcast" (1 Sm 1:18). Finally, in the eyes of her society and herself, Hannah would be a "complete" woman, even though in the bargain she had dedicated her son to the Lord. After weaning, she kept her vow and left Samuel to be raised by the priest, Eli.

Pregnancy may or may not heighten the eroticism between a couple, but every individual has certain areas that take on highly erotic significance. Usually this is the result of learning and experience more than any inborn, preset pattern. People sometimes make assumptions about rumored "hot" spots and are often disappointed to find out they must either be poor technicians or else their partner "just isn't made right!"

A man or woman can be confused if their body doesn't work the way they perceive everyone else's does. Movies are particularly troublesome for insinuating that all a lover has to do is "touch the right body part" and "nirvana" is just around the corner. When what's around the corner turns out to be a dead-end wall, more than egos falter.

Breasts are a good illustration of the problem of false assumptions about the way the body responds. Only a few women report experiencing orgasm through breast manipulation alone. Finding pleasure in breast fondling is quite variable among women. Yet ninety-nine percent of men report manually manipulating the breast in foreplay, believing that their partners are as erotically stimulated by it as they are.[5] My husband once overheard a conversation among a group of nurses about breast stimulation. Said one, "I hate having my breasts touched. I told Roger when we were dating that was for marriage." "What do you say now that you are married?" asked another. "Oh, now I tell him, 'Those are for children!'"

The reluctance to share how one really feels is typical with sexual issues. The underlying belief is that a "real" woman would love such behavior from a man. Such a bias serves to keep a woman from freely communicating since sharing areas of inadequacy is naturally difficult.

SEX IS FOR THE HEALTHY

Today we have a new reason to loathe the body and to see it as unhealthy. The latest statistics warn us of the increased number of sexual partners that individuals are likely to have today, thus greatly increasing the odds of contracting a sexually transmitted disease.

My husband is a physician. He has seen an increase in his practice of divorcées in their forties or fifties who are discovering times have changed—the hard way. Many are angry and hurt that their second partnership may have resulted in a disease. The outcome for many is shame and a sense of dirtiness that can linger beyond the sheer physical effects. Of course, in the case of condyloma and herpes recurrent episodes painfully remind a person they are diseased for a lifetime.

Feeling diseased and dirty sometimes has nothing to do with a physical illness, but is the consequence of feeling worthless. The result may be increased sexual activity that is demeaning or unfulfilling. "This is what I and my devalued body deserve." Others are unable to experience pleasure through the same body that has been the source of guilt, humiliation, and pain.

Rebecca felt that way. She hated sex. Her husband of two years couldn't have been kinder or more loving, but his patience was growing thin. He did not know that from the time she was three, Rebecca had been molested by her father. She only vaguely remembered the details and had made a sincere effort to forgive him. As far as she was concerned, it was a closed chapter in her life. Consequently, Rebecca was furious when her doctor suggested that since her problems were not physical, perhaps there were some unresolved issues that she needed to address. She never returned, ignored his recommendation to see a counselor, and eventually divorced.

David's lovemaking was quick and business-like. He hated being touched. His wife's loving efforts to reach out to him literally left him in a cold sweat. So had his sister when she used to come into his room when he was a child to caress and fondle his body.

Rebecca and David are two of thousands of adult children whose bodies have been violated, and who consequently have become uncomfortable with sensuous touch and normal body response even in appropriate settings. The same reaction is not unusual among rape survivors, men and women who have suffered physical abuse, and those who have had abortions.

Kathryn is an example of those who respond by seemingly embracing the sensual. She had long ago lost count of the number of her sexual encounters. Her father introduced her to sex and she had learned quickly that she could use it to manipulate men. Kathryn reasoned that since it was going to happen anyway, she might as well be in control. That fantasy came crashing down on her thirtieth birthday. She found herself trying to cope with urges to mutilate and hurt her own body which had caused her so much grief.

Doreen faced a very real physical problem. Her legs had failed to develop normally. In combination with several other physical problems, this deformity left her feeling insecure about her lovability. Fearful that she would not been seen as the normal, healthy girl she was, Doreen became an outrageous flirt.

A "reaping and sowing" sermon suddenly made her stop and realize how many sexual partners she had had—miraculously without disease. Doreen immediately entered counseling to understand the overwhelming need she felt to bed any "nice" guy who was willing. What she discovered was that each partner made her feel whole and even superior since she had become a skilled and responsive lover... at least for a while. Doreen's compulsion for sex was really a way of dealing with a poor body image.

In a society that suggests the young have all the fun, the reality of getting old can be equated with being unhealthy. Shirley, who is fifty, and Bob at fifty-five, have taken to going to bed at different times. Neither has been able to talk to the other about how disturbed they are with the changes they have noticed in their sexual response. Both have silently concluded what the media have so effectively promoted: sex is not for the old, disabled, or unhealthy.

For a while they thought they had staved off the effects of aging. Both were involved in exercise programs and Shirley diligently used anti-aging cosmetics and worked at looking attractive. But the truth could not be denied: Bob's erection simply wasn't as firm as it used to be and Shirley lacked lubrication. Clearly, they were no longer able to produce the erotic response in one another they used to enjoy.

Shirley and Bob's conclusion seriously diminished their pleasure in their marriage and made them vulnerable to an affair. Was it really their age? Was it him? Or her? Since sex is rarely openly discussed, they had not learned that the bodily responses that appeared to herald the end of their sexual relationship were normal signs of aging. These changes in no way were a measure of their continuing interest and love for one another. Instead of adapting to them, they began to view themselves as old and therefore unhealthy, allowing their unspoken fears to drive a wedge into what had always been a close relationship.

YOU CAN CREATE A SEXY BODY IF YOU WORK HARD ENOUGH

People like Bob, Shirley, Rebecca, and Doreen and countless others suffer deeply as they struggle to understand and use their bodies in ways that enhance their worth and personal body image. It is not "just a body" that is violated when sex is misused or misunderstood. The totality of who a person is has been affected. Attempts to dismiss the sexual act as simple physical release, just plain fun and pleasure, or as a biological necessity ignores its larger significance.

No amount of cosmetics, body building, or even natural beauty can guarantee good sex or a healthy body image. A responsive, healthy body has more to do with proper understanding than what a person's body looks like or how it operates. Our body image is influenced by what happens between us and others, but most significantly, what happens between our own two ears.

To some, you can create a sexy body without working very hard at all. You just take off your clothes. Clothes convey two conflicting messages. On the one hand, they are used to enhance the appeal of our body. On the other, they prevent disgust, shame, or disapproval. What is considered sexy is determined by factors that are predominately body-oriented or predominately social depending on the culture. In the West, nudity is closely associated with sex. Not so with the Aborigine in Australia and many others. To see an Aborigine nude, even defecating, would not be embarrassing or sexual in their culture. However, great shame would result if you were to come upon that same person eating.

What is immodest is very culturally defined. In the past, an Arab peasant woman might have thrown her skirt up to protect her face from prying Western eyes, thereby revealing other areas that make *us* far more nervous. When dresses were cut low during the eighteenth century, a woman was humiliated to have the ankle or the point of the shoulder exposed. Naked tribesmen frequently add clothes when courting or when involved with fertility dances. Missionaries were surprised to discover that covering bodies that had always been uncovered triggered sexual desires instead of discouraging them. As one sage humorously noted, "Prudery, it seems, provides mankind with endless aphrodisiacs, hence, no doubt, the reluctance to abandon it."

Removing clothes is actually an almost universal sign of respect. In Europe a man might tilt his hat to show deference for someone. A Moslem will remove their shoes to worship. A servant does not wear more elaborate or more abundant layers of clothes than his master. Would you outdress your boss at an important meeting?

No discussion of the body creates more controversy than the appropriateness of nudity. Modern sun worshipers maintain their lives are enriched when "the constant pressure of curiosity is removed; then all sorts of repressions, fixations, and other unhealthy mental stresses simply disappear."[6] Nudists are correct about one thing: being surrounded with nude bodies does desensitize people, just as the missionaries discovered. The nude dancer loses her erotic clout compared to the dancer who teasingly uses clothes or fans in her act and leaves something to the imagination.

The question remains: is becoming a nudist the *preferred* way to deal with the body and the associated feelings of shame, curiosity, and arousal? Extreme modesty reflects the attitude that the body is inherently shameful and a stimulant to uncontrollable desires. What qualifies as extreme? In our society, it might perhaps be categorized as always making love with the lights out, never undressing in front of others in an appropriate setting, or punishing children for normal curiosity about the body.

My husband recalls never seeing his mother or sisters nude as he was growing up. Accidental sightings were accompanied by screams and slamming doors. As a teenager, he and his buddies were obsessed with the possibility of glimpsing someone of the opposite sex nude... or even just one naked part. This was not healthy, but neither is the blasé attitude of many of today's teens. They have seen so many nude bodies on television and in the movies that they are no longer impressed by the beauty and the mystery of the body.

Nudity titillates because it inevitably makes us think of sex. Nudity is not sex and is not shameful in itself. But Westerners have a tradition of viewing the body with shame. After the Fall, Adam and Eve "knew they were naked." They were self-conscious and uncomfortable about being nude and immediately set about making themselves clothes (Gn 3:7). When Noah exposed himself, his youngest son made an issue of seeing his father's genitals and was chastised for his attitude. The two older sons respectfully covered Noah (Gn 9:21-24). David's wife, Michal, complained bitterly to him that he had behaved disgracefully by dancing nude in the street and exposing himself to the onlookers (2 Sm 6:14, 20).

Clearly, public nudity was perceived as shameful in the biblical world. It was used as a means of humiliation during war (2 Sm 10:4-5; Is 20:4; 47:3). Interestingly, the Lord commanded Isaiah to go naked—which may have meant wearing only the undertunic—and barefoot for three years as a warning sign to the Egyptians that they would be prisoners of war (Is 20:3).

Today, public nudity still makes news. The theater production of *Hair* left the audience stunned when nude actors appeared in a mainline production. Streakers continue to plague large crowds and even Prince Andrew's nude swimming romp and Princess Stephanie's biweekly topless romps make the headlines. As with the ancients, a touch of shame and embarrassment continues to permeate our psyche when confronted with the naked human body.

Adam and Eve originally felt no shame with nudity (Gn 2:25). In their innocence they gazed upon each other's bodies and found pleasure and beauty with no discomfort. Nudity itself was nothing to be feared when it lacked the direct link to sex we seemed compelled to give it. When they lost their innocence, they were suddenly "naked and ashamed."

Could it be that our discomfort with nudity and our sexuality is related? Is the eye with which it is seen part of the problem most of us have in accepting our bodies? Scripture suggests that is the case: "To the pure, all things are pure, but to those who are corrupted and do not believe, nothing is pure" (Ti 1:15).

In primitive societies the body, sex, and religion were closely identified and expressed through religious myth and ritual. The Hebrew tradition always considered sex and birth as part of God's plan. The truth is, sex permeates all of human experience by virtue of our being created as two sexes. Men and women are drawn to one another because of and in spite of their differences. As confusing and challenging as that might be, it fuels eroticism.

As the early Christian church became more and more institutionalized, it moved farther and farther from its early Judeo roots. The spiritual became superior, while "the flesh"—sex and the body—were viewed as more earthy and common. Such a nonbiblical but widely accepted separation has resulted in a great deal of pain and confusion. Hopefully we will find therein the impetus to again reunite religion and sex and view the human body with the totality it was meant to have.

Just as with other attempts at self-improvement, the distraction of struggling to be the best at sex enables us to deceive ourselves. We can come to believe nothing is really amiss inside or with our relationships. We can choose to focus on external efforts to remain young and beautiful and increase our sex appeal. The inevitable aging process usually catches up with these shallow goals. There is certainly more to life than sex, and more to the body than being sexy. We will consider the overlooked answer in the last chapter.

REFLECTION

Take a walk down memory lane alone or with a significant other. Remember how you first learned about sex. How old were you? Did the knowledge leave you awestruck? Frightened? Turned on? Repulsed? When your body began to show the first signs of puberty were you excited about it or embarrassed? How were the facts of life presented to you? How did this presentation affect the way you viewed your body? Did your parents ignore your developing sexuality or did they affirm or make you ashamed of it?

TAKING INVENTORY I

1. List five things you do to enhance your sex appeal.

2. Do you believe you would be a better lover if you lost weight, firmed up, or could have some plastic surgery? If the answer is yes, why do you feel it would make a difference?

3. Are you fearful that aging will negatively affect your sexual life?

4. If you have sought ways to improve your sexual life, has it included taking a hard look at your relationship, ability to communicate, and your attitude toward your body?

TAKING INVENTORY II

1. Things I think my partner *likes* about my body:
    a.
    b.
    c.

2. Things I think my partner *dislikes* about my body:
    a.
    b.
    c.

3. Things I like about my body:
    a.
    b.
    c.

4. Things I dislike about my body:
    a.
    b.
    c.

5. I could be more sensuous if:

5

Gender in Question

THE ONLY FEMALE COMPETITOR who did not have to undergo a test to confirm her gender at the Montreal Olympics in 1976 was Princess Anne. That such a test would be required seems strange. Gender has historically been pretty simple. You are either a man or a woman. But there are people for whom something so seemingly obvious is not so simple.

Each and every one of us can likely name a time when we became insecure about our body image as a male or female. Our genitals spoke loudly but our minds wondered. Such musings were usually momentary, the result of being completely ignored by the cutest girl in school or stood up on a Saturday night. For some, the questioning extends through a season of life.

Gender identity means the awareness that we are one sex and not the other. It is not confusion over roles and expectations. For most of us, the truth that we were a boy or a girl occurred between eighteen and thirty-six months. How we *feel* about being male or female is independent of *knowing* "I am a boy" or "I am a girl."

Our self-image as male or female is highly influenced by what we see. While genetic factors and hormonal mistakes are possible, it has never been proven that either provide more than a "push" toward homosexuality. Learning and socialization provide the additional impetus for those who are biologically sensitive and serve as the major factors in development of homosexuality for individuals whose biology is intact. For some men and women, the "push" consists solely of their own free will to choose a lifestyle that is at odds with the majority.

SONIA AND DAVID

Sonia recounts how as an infant she was separated from her mother as a result of a serious infection. This separation interrupted the normal bonding and nourishing of the mother-child relationship. Upon entering preschool, a female teacher singled Sonia out for private "punishment" that in reality was sexual molestation.

Instinctively sensing that something bad was happening, she began to associate being female with shame and violation. Sonia coped by dreaming of the day that she would grow up and become a man.[1] Belief by a gender-disturbed child that he or she is or will actually *become* the opposite sex appears to be related to age. Older children are less likely to express such a desire.[2]

At two, David became fascinated with his mother's long hair. He sometimes mimicked her by placing a towel on his head. Enrolled in a playschool of almost all girls, he began to carry a tote, pretending it was a purse. David expressed desires to dress in his mother's clothes and jewelry. His feminine behavior and body movement escalated with the birth of a sister and his verbalized feelings that she was now the preferred child. The little boy loved dolls, particularly Barbie, and dreamed of being a ballerina. David slept fitfully and would wander into his parent's room in the middle of the night to ask if they loved only his sister or if they loved him too.[3]

Sonia and David's early experiences provided a "push" toward gender confusion. Sonia continued to pursue a masculine image. Inside she struggled with the shame over other incidences of abuse, her own self-hatred, feelings of detachment, and the core need she had to recognize who she was. As a teen Sonia entered into a relationship in which she acted out her masculine role. "This experience, although fulfilling and pleasant in a way, only seemed to underscore the emptiness inside... the essential rift between the feminine beauty I wanted to unite with and the virtues of a mysterious womanly person who was hidden on the inside, a person I was altogether unaware of and unwilling to acknowledge but who represented the real, integrated self."[4]

It is too soon to tell what will happen with David. Will he become a transvestite? A transsexual or a homosexual? The odds are increased that David will be gay. Studies verify that homosexual men and women are involved in more cross-gender behavior as children than heterosexuals.[5]

The complexity of developing appropriate gender identity is illustrated through these stories. Early factors contributed to identity confusion and insecurity. They could easily look back—as many in the gay community do—and remember always feeling gay. Earliest memories may well be of cross-gender behavior or a preoccupation with the same sex.

These kinds of memories do not prove, however, that homosexuality is biologically based. Such proof simply does not exist, despite periodic publishing of "definitive studies" that have so far been impossible to reproduce or lacking in some other way. Such recollections do provide insight into the variety of factors that begin to orient and motivate a child toward homosexuality and rejection of a body image that is in line with their genetics.

Should you panic when your little Johnny or Joanie raids the opposite-sex parent's closet for a new wardrobe? Most children play at cross-dressing as a normal and natural part of childhood. I remember begging my mother to buy me an undershirt and some jockey shorts. Did I want to be a boy? You bet! At the tender age of five I had figured out that boys had more fun, got to do more than girls, and wore clothes that were a great deal more comfortable for climbing trees.

Today most people would categorize me as "feminine." Indeed, one of my passions in life is to help women feel good about themselves because of the very fact they are female. Like most kids, my foray into the realm of the opposite sex didn't have much to do with confusion over whether I was a boy or girl. I just wanted to have more fun.

The line is indeed fine between children who have true clinically defined cross-gender problems and those whose behavior simply falls outside what we see happening with most kids. One small boy may have a strong identification with and preference for the sex-typed characteristics of the opposite sex. He can sometimes be hard to distinguish from one who does not wish to be a girl and who is not excessively interested in feminine things, but who doesn't seem to fit in with male peer groups.

Perhaps a boy doesn't like rough and tumble play or sports and is not highly motivated to play with masculine toys. One should not jump to the conclusion that the problem is a clinical cross-gender one. He may not feel very masculine or be good at what boys do. He will probably have a low opinion of himself as a result.[6] His self-image might be further damaged by playmates, siblings, or parents who may label him a "sissy," "wimp," or "fairy." Girls are far less likely to be stigmatized by being called a "tomboy." They enjoy greater latitude in how they experience their gender, without damaging labels.

What is masculine or feminine, like attractiveness, is difficult to define. People know it when they see it and beauty can really be in the eye of the beholder. Anyone who falls outside of what the majority feels is acceptable or who is on the fringe is usually aware of it. The misfits will be subject to stereotypical discrimination and labeling.

Not measuring up—whether real or imagined—prompts

attempts to compensate. Some people adopt hyper male or female stances. "How dare you suggest I have a problem! I've gone to bed with more people than you can count." "When those 'queers' came to town, I knocked a few heads." Others, like the actor who plays Pee Wee Herman, exhibit what they have—perhaps hoping the reaction they elicit will convince others but mostly themselves they are more than adequate.

Clearly no one event seals the lid on sexual orientation. Traumas at crucial times in our life—such as timing of puberty, abuse, athletic ability, big or slight builds, talents, over-sensitivity, sibling interactions, and peer relationships—are just a handful of influences that at the right time can cause confusion about being a man or woman.

People with gender disorders may or may not be involved with the same sex. Persons without apparent gender disorders can become homosexual. Recognition that sexual orientation and/or gender disturbances are the result of many complex factors leaves the door open for change. Some homosexual individuals exit the gay lifestyle. People who appear to completely reject their gender for a while sometimes change. Such reversals offer further proof that sexual orientation is not necessarily set in stone.

Even secular studies—whose natural bias is that sexual reorientation is impossible or at least unwise—report success rates between thirty-three and sixty percent.[7] Christian groups are more likely to believe in the possibility of supernatural intervention and healing and be highly motivated to help people honor God in their sexual behavior. They report even higher rates of fifty to ninety percent.[8] Those who oppose such intervention continue to insist "there is no cure."

MILD DISCONTENT TO COMPLETE REJECTION

Frank quietly and carefully slid the drawer back into the dresser. The house seemed strangely still in contrast to his wildly beating heart. He glanced in the mirror before leaving the bedroom. A blob of blue eyeliner clung accusingly under his right eye. He grabbed a tissue and removed the last vestige of proof of his secret double life. Cynthia was just coming into the house. "Hi, Hon," he called, trying to sound casual, "you're back early."

No one who knew Frank would have believed his "hobby." Afterall, he was the former terror of the neighborhood. Nothing too serious, just the "boys will be boys" variety of trouble. Lots of people remembered what a good athlete he was. No aspect of Frank's adult behavior or career choice would give anyone a clue he was a cross-dresser... a transvestite.

Dressing in women's clothes began in childhood, when a teenage cousin visited and stayed in his room. He had never before seen women's underwear. It was soft and beautiful and he had fun "trying it on for size." Frank was mortified the day his cousin walked in and found him standing in front of the mirror in *her* bra and undies. Taking particular delight in his vulnerability, she insisted he model for her or she would tell his mother.

Despite the humiliation and perhaps fueled by it, Frank's fascination continued. As opportunity and circumstance arose, he borrowed articles of clothing belonging to his mother or sister. In the beginning his feelings were of generalized excitement, but one day as he was slipping on a pair of pantyhose, he ejaculated. Masturbation became a part of his routine as had the fantasy of being female. In fact, envisioning himself as a woman was an important part of his arousal mechanism with his wife, although she knew nothing of it.

Frank tried on numerous occasions to stop cross-dressing, but the resultant depression and uneasiness always broke down his resolve. Slipping into something feminine was so comforting. This intense feeling of comfort will continue and perhaps even increase his desire to dress as he gets older, even if sexual arousal is no longer a part of the experience.

Despite his fantasies of being a woman, Frank's desire for a female sex partner will not change. Histories of transvestites tell us that fifty percent of them recall cross-dressing before puberty.[9] Their preference for undergarments is different from others, with even greater gender problems among those who prefer to cross-dress in outerwear.

Someone like Frank is different from the person who rejects his body. Although early histories appear similar, commonly in their thirties, a male who more completely repudiates his sex often expresses a desire to live more openly and consistently as a woman. Typically, he will leave his marriage and seek a sex-change operation.

Why the classic transvestite does not experience this escalation is unknown. Clinically, such an individual suffers from *gender dysphoria*: a general discontent with one's biological sex, the desire to be regarded as the opposite sex, and to possess the body of the opposite sex.[10]

Its most extreme form is *transsexualism*: the complete rejection of one's body as a man or woman. Among transsexuals, there is no greater example of this than the individual who not only rejects his or her body but also his or her sexual orientation. The homosexual transsexual or gender dysphoric considers the appropriate love object a person who they perceive as being the opposite sex, but who is in reality the same biological sex.

As children, men who grow up to be transsexuals tend to dislike physical competitiveness and prefer playing with girls and dolls. Women suffering from this syndrome typically reject any game, activity, or dress that appear feminine. Such a history is almost always found in the true transsexual. But remember, people who appear feminine as a young boy or masculine as a young girl do not always grow up to be transsexual. The majority of feminine boys do become homosexual, but they rarely reject their body and maleness as completely as the transsexual.[11]

Sexually, the male homosexual transsexual hates his genitals, hides them when having sex, and is reluctant to have them touched. A partner who was too interested in the trans-sexual's male genitalia would be rejected and labeled "homo-sexual." Likewise, the transsexual woman desires a feminine partner who has no history of homosexual behavior. She dislikes being touched on the breasts or vulva. Puberty creates great anxiety for such a girl because the reality of breasts and periods mean she can no longer ignore the fact that she is a woman.

Considerable controversy has surrounded the appropriate-ness of surgery on a healthy body to bring it in line with a psychological disorder. Since genitals are the symbol of their despised sex, it is no surprise that their removal is requested first.

Perry Desmond reports how he spent years and fortunes trying to perfect his womanly image. His goal was to "correct God's drastic mistake." Billed as "The South's Most Beautiful Boy," he used massive doses of hormones for thirteen years to enlarge his hips and bust. Silicon injections perfected his feminine look and eventual removal of his male organs com-pleted the job. The anticipated relief of ridding himself of the last vestige of maleness did not materialize. Desmond reflects, "All I had done was chop up my body. I had ex-pected the world would change; everything would be differ-ent. But that's not the way it is." He asks, "If a person decided he was a monkey, would they graft on fur and add a tail?"[12]

The scientific literature reports few female gender dys-phorics who are not homosexual. One exception tells of a woman who remembers she and her sisters "playing boys." She thoroughly enjoyed the game and even fantasized about it when not playing it, but reports no "tomboy" or other strong cross-gender practices. In fact, she looked forward to puberty. Her fantasy life, however, involved erotic scenes of men and boys. She dated a man her father warned her "seemed homosexual." That made him all the more appeal-ing and they were together for ten years. Whenever they had intercourse she wore a shirt to hide her breasts and pre-tended she was a boy.

By age twenty-two she acknowledged that her "fantasies of homosexual men were not going away." This woman then began dressing like a man and joined the homosexual community as a "gay man." The idea of men being aroused by other men was very erotic and appealing to her. At age twenty-eight she had a mastectomy and took hormones, followed later by extensive genital surgery. A new long-term relationship was established and she and her male lover were viewed as a "gay" couple. Being diagnosed with AIDS, for her, was perversely positive. "No, I have never regretted changing my sex even for a second, despite my AIDS diagnosis, and in some... way feel that my condition is proof that I really attained my goal of being a gay man—even to the finish, I am with my gay brothers."[13]

CANNIBAL COMPULSION

Sometimes the motivation behind a body image disturbance is not rejection of one's sex but infusion with it. There are those who seek a "a shot of masculinity" or a "dose of femininity" vicariously, from their sexual encounters. Acquiring some trait from one who is seen as having it in plentiful supply is reminiscent of the cannibal. Cannibals don't eat their victims because they are hungry. They eat parts or all of a captive because it enables them to feel powerful or they hope to acquire some element they sense is lacking or in short supply in themselves.

Poor body image motivates some homosexuals to search for "prey" that will supply what is missing. Leanne Payne illustrates this cannibal compulsion in *The Healing of the Homosexual.*[14] Michael was a successful and bright young man who felt trapped between his desire to live up to the tenets of his Christian faith and the overwhelming desire he felt for a male acquaintance. He described his friend as "good looking, successful, and smart." Michael was helped in therapy to see that the traits he admired were his own disowned traits.

Having never been affirmed by his family, he sought in another what he thought were missing parts of himself. Once he was able to accept a truly accurate body image, the power of his compulsive thoughts and fantasies was broken.

And then there was Stan, whose small stature put him on the edge of what our society deems masculine. His craving of athletic body types and fantasies of male genitals under-scored the lack of masculinity he felt. Stan was starving for this masculinity and could hardly get his fill of strong, ath-letic men.

His friend Bill was attracted to men with big hairy chests. His only memory of a father who had died in the war was of cuddling next to his naked, warm chest. His sexual encoun-ters were a search for safer times, comfort, and the feeling of being loved and accepted. Although these men must accept responsibility for their behavior, none were originally moti-vated by lust—rather from a need that should and could have been met in a more appropriate way.

THE CONFUSION OF GENDER

Are there differences between men and women who suffer from gender dysphoria and/or homosexuality? The fact of a woman's more passive sexual role makes it easier for her to marry and have a child, reinforcing her femininity in her own and society's eyes. Although the element of abuse is high in the early histories of both male and female homo-sexuals, it is a particularly salient factor in lesbianism.

The different approaches to sex among heterosexual men and women are also found among homosexuals. It is not uncommon for a lesbian relationship to grow out of a close emotional relationship. Convinced they are understood bet-ter, more intimate, and valued in a way they have never expe-rienced with a man makes stepping over the line physically appear right—because it "feels" so right. By contrast, male homosexuals approach relationships much like the male heterosexual, with an eye to the physical.

All human beings desire relationship, including those who struggle with accepting their body in the fullness of its masculinity or femininity. Longing for intimacy is normal and healthy. Ideally we find it first in rich, rewarding, accepting, affirming experiences with our parents. Then we yearn for its expression in its most personal sense with a partner whose *very opposition* enriches and deepens the experience.

Such is God's design. To settle for less impedes the fullness of what it means to be a man or woman. Religious professor Oliver O'Donovan states it well: "Other relationships, however important in themselves and however rich in intimacy and fidelity, do not disclose the meaning of biological nature in this way. They float, as it were, like oil upon water, suspended upon bodily existence rather than growing out of it."[15]

Like it or not, we come into the world as two sexes designed for heterosexual union and the possibility of procreation. Although the details of marriage are not spelled out, it is designed around this biological fact. An intimate and lifelong union offers possibilities and enrichments that are beyond the ordinary. True communion occurs between two people who were designed to complete each other.

Our most basic body image, that of being a male or female, has been twisted for some. Others have a strong sense of themselves as men or women, but distort their relationships with the opposite sex and reduce them to sex objects. Some live in ways that are unbalanced or that deny important aspects of who they are. Children are sexually assaulted by those whose insecurities about their bodies are worked out through the grossest violations. Clearly, the effects of not having a healthy body image in the area of our sexuality are severe, with societal, spiritual, and solitary repercussions.

"WHEN I'M ALONE, I'M IN BAD COMPANY"

This country-western song title captures the utter loneliness of someone with a poor self-image. There is no more dramatic illustration of the futility of believing that changing the external self will result in self-acceptance than those with gender identity problems.

As we have already discussed, exaggerated behavior and attempts to transform the body result in even greater distortions of identity. At first the energy and activity of beginning such a course lowers anxiety, but soon the very effort needed to sustain a self-improvement crusade serves to reinforce the feelings of unacceptability. Anxiety increases and activity escalates, but the possibility of living life without such dramatic measures is still not reevaluated.

Having jumped on a treadmill, the person feels like there is no way to get off and no alternative. Because little time has been designated to looking inward, the inner life becomes shallow and superficial. The focus is no longer *life* but *lifestyle.* All one's attention is directed toward how life is lived rather than on living it.

The gender dysphoric can easily be dismissed as someone to be pitied but not someone with whom we can identify. The choices he or she makes, however, are prompted by the same insecurity that motivates the rest of us—I don't fit or measure up. We all share the belief that in order to be accepted and loved we must change. We all need to be aware of the things we do that are inspired by the lack of acceptance of who we are.

PERSONAL HISTORY PART II

There are no right or wrong answers for this section. The questions are designed to help you become aware of the messages you received as a child regarding your gender. Even though men and women have more traits in common than ones that are different, they are not "exactly" alike except for genitals. As you think about these questions, distinguish between your gender identity—the sense of being a male or female—and how you feel about it. If these questions stir memories that are upsetting and/or need resolution, do not hesitate to discuss them with a competent, trustworthy person.

1. What kind of messages did your dad or other significant men in your life convey to you about being a man or woman by:

    a. the way they treated and talked about women?

    b. the way they treated and talked about men?

2. What did you learn from your mother about what it was like to be a woman?

3. Was it OK in your family to be different from your same-sex parent?

4. Did you grow up thinking any part of your body was disgusting? If so, how did you get that idea?

5. Were you labeled by other kids, teachers, or family members in a way that suggested you were not very masculine or feminine?

6. Is your relationship with your same-sex parent a good one? If not, when did it first seem to get into trouble?

7. Are the people you attract ones that affirm your femininity or masculinity in healthy ways?

8. Were you the sex your parents wanted?

9. If you struggle with your sexuality, is there a chance you were sexually molested by strangers, friends, or family?

10. Since few adults in the nineties have had more than a piecemeal sexual education, have you made a *sincere* effort to educate yourself about sexual anatomy, physiology, and healthy functioning? If not, why?

6

The Battle of the Bulge

*B*EING OBSESSED WITH WEIGHT is a relatively new phenomenon. Packing a few extra pounds has previously served as a built-in calling card that announced: "I have plenty to eat. I'm wealthy." In fact, if a woman wanted to be in the king's harem of the Karagwe of East Africa, her main objective would be to become very fat. If she were a member of the Ekoi tribe of Nigeria, her father might prepare her for marriage by sending her to a fattening house. Kept in seclusion, the bride-to-be would be fed fatty foods and allowed no physical exertion until she waddled out one year later.

But losing weight and fitness to the extreme have become American pastimes. Books that tell us how to take it off fast, slow, or forever, are currently the biggest sellers in the bookstores with the exception of the Bible. Three billion dollars were spent on dieting in 1990 alone.

Those heralders of the public pulse, the tabloids, are filled with news of "Kirstie Alley's Secret Torment is making her Eat, and Eat, and Eat" and of Farrah Fawcett kicking Ryan O'Neal out of bed for being overweight. The January 1991 issue of *People* magazine pictured Oprah Winfrey on the cover declaring, "I'll never diet again." Barbara Walters invited Delta Burke to be on the same show as Shirley MacLaine and Mel Gibson, a decision made not because of equal status but of weight.

At the same time, we have a presidential First Lady who dares to be herself. Her refusal to partake in facelifts, hair dying, or diets has not prevented her from becoming one of the most highly respected presidential wives in decades. Barbara Bush is indeed a rare woman. She has what *Allure* magazine's editor calls "beauty with personality, accomplishment and ability"—in contrast to "beauty" which implies perfection and blandness.[1]

Most of us would refuse to change our politics, taste in music, or favorite foods because of external pressure to do so. Unlike Mrs. Bush, many of us readily put ourselves through a lifetime of struggle to conform to the current vogue of lean bodies.

BEATING THE BODY INTO SHAPE

Although some still considered it "vulgar amusement," the first golf and tennis tournaments for women paved the way in the 1800s for feminine fitness and weight control. Sixteen-inch Indian clubs were popular, but it was highly recommended that they be flung and circled only in the privacy of the bedroom.

With the new century came new ideas. Women were spotted in the first clingy bathing suits. Weighing one and a half pounds when wet, swimming in them did double-duty for fitness. Tennis was still the rage, although playing in corsets that left one bleeding and sore was not for everyone. The more delicate could take the advice found in *Vogue* magazine and "pirouette while you peel potatoes."[2] Women competed in the 1920 Olympics and enjoyed folk dancing, but were taught at Swarthmore College to develop upper body strength in this manner: "Turn on the vacuum cleaner. Bend from the waist and push vacuum cleaner back and forth... keep head up, back straight. Repeat until carpet is clean."[3]

Exercise machines which appeared in 1930 were recommended for the young. *Today's Health* magazine cautioned the middle-aged, "These people lack either the sense or the courage to admit that they are growing older and that former activity is becoming increasingly fatiguing."[4] In March 1990, two hundred thousand athletes fifty-five and older competed in "Senior Games" organized by the U.S. National Senior Sports Organization. Apparently the recommended "... progressive decrease in bodily exertion" was not necessary after all.

In the forties, women's exercise remained primarily in the home. For hips and posture, the *Ladies' Home Journal* suggested "holding a bundle of folded laundry, walk up the stairs. Keep back straight. Step firmly on balls of the feet. Repeat twenty times daily." In 1957, *Mademoiselle* recommended firming up the chin by balancing the wooden end of a broom vertically on the chin for thirty minutes per day for a couple of weeks... or until they came to lock you up, we might add.

In the sixties, a Palm Springs spa advised women to exercise their facial muscles by working a rubber band down from just under the nose to the throat and repeat until the rubber burned. Women became joggers and dancers in the seventies. The eighties began a push for exercise to become a lifestyle rather than a fad. With the aging population and aerobically damaged knees of the nineties, women are into low impact workouts, walking, fitness without exercise. The latest book on fitness recommends gardening.[5] History has a way of coming full circle.

STRIVING TO BE BARBIE

Barbie's thin, flawless body and never-ending legs have appealed to girls since 1959, with sales of seven hundred million dollars in 1990. Remove her latest couture fashion and you find a "strangely eroticized piece of plastic."[6] *Allure* magazine gives this apt description of the Barbie doll: "Stretched out nude with her wholesome bland smile, her flowing flaxen hair teasing the tips of those sturdy voluptuous breasts, her fastidious little feet permanently poised for high heels, she's Hugh Hefner's dream centerfold, the airbrushed, antiseptic girl-next-door with 'a bod for sin.'..."[7]

Barbie's incorrect politics means she is now facing new competition! A realistically proportioned doll with wider waist, larger feet, shorter neck and legs, is just hitting the market. The new "Happy to Be Me" doll is the brainchild of Cathy Meredig, president of High Self-Esteem Toys. Her goal is to "help young girls develop realistic body images and accept themselves as they are."

Meredig's decision to develop an alternative to Barbie was spurred by the alarming statistics on women and their bodies: two percent become anorexic; fifteen percent bulimic; and seventy percent believe they are overweight. None of her friends felt good about themselves despite their accomplishments. Meredig complains, "What they're trying to sell to little girls is a very dead-end fairy tale, which is that you have to be thin and sexy to be loved and accepted."[8] It will be interesting to see if young girls will make the change.

Young and old alike are fascinated with idealized beauty. *People* magazine put out an extra edition entitled, "The Fifty Most Beautiful People in the World, 1991." The writer of the essays ventures this explanation as to why the "chosen ones" deserve to be revered and why we so willingly plunk down our offering to read about them: "There's an ideal these people illustrate, it's close to what the mystics used to call grace... a certain power, a knowing. Beautiful people are energized by this self-knowledge. It's a dangerous thing of course. The rest of us fall for it every time."[9]

We do indeed. A 1984 *Glamour* survey reported that their readers would rather lose ten to fifteen pounds than succeed at work or love. What a dangerous priority! If we play it all out with Barbie, will it come true for us? Will our lives work better if we study the beautiful people? If our problem is overweight, will thin really be the answer?

We have stated repeatedly that people who enjoy high self-esteem have a good body image despite the shape of their body. However, people who are overweight—or who think they are—almost inevitably have low self-esteem and a poor body image. They are far more likely to think of themselves in nonsexual terms and to fear disapproval. Even doctors have been shown to be prejudiced against the obese.

We find it hard to feel good about ourselves with extra pounds. Perhaps that is why Kirstie, Ryan, Delta, and Oprah make the headlines. "If they can't do it with all they have going for them, maybe I can feel better about my weight," we tell ourselves. When we believe that having a figure like Barbie is the magic potion for happiness, love, and acceptance, being overweight can be depressing. Barring a clear and evident medical problem, being heavy is considered weak-willed.

An obese person is usually stigmatized over their entire lifespan. Stereotyping starts early. Researchers showed pictures of a variety of children to their peers and asked them to rank who they might like to be friends with. Fat children were chosen last. Physically handicapped children were perceived as more desirable than the overweight child.[10] Studies also tell us that being overweight affects educational and occupational opportunities. The TV show *Lifeline* recently reported fifty percent less chance of acceptance to a prestigious college for someone overweight.

Although both sexes suffer the ill effects of excess fat, women's social relationships are more seriously disrupted. They date less often and endure more criticism from other women. Husbands are twelve times more likely to criticize their wives about weight than the wives are likely to criticize their husbands.

Even though the social consequences of being fat can

affect psychological adjustment and self-esteem, the over-weight are not prone to be more clinically psychologically disturbed when viewed over a lifetime.[11] Attractiveness is statistically unrelated to measures of well-being such as self-esteem. Behavioral differences, however, do smack of self-fulfilling prophecy.

In one study, college kids were able to accurately judge the attractiveness of people they talked to on the telephone but could not see.[12] Those perceived as thin were judged more socially skilled and likable. The more obese a person was, the poorer the impression. Worse still, the heaviest subjects made the person they were talking to feel socially inadequate. With a history of social rejection or outright cruelty, the obese run a greater risk of developing poor social skills. Expecting rejection can result in adopting dislikable behaviors, setting up a vicious cycle for those with a poor body image.

THE MODERN DAY DISEASE

In her book, *The Beauty Myth*, Naomi Wolf introduces the segment on eating disorders by graphically describing anorexia: "There is a disease spreading. It taps on the shoulder America's firstborn sons, its best and brightest. At its touch, they turn from food. Their bones swell out from receding flesh. Shadows invade their faces.... What is happening to the fine young men, in their brush cuts and khaki trousers? It hurts to look at them."[13]

By ascribing this eating disorder to young men instead of women, Wolf makes a powerful point. If the best and bright-est *males* were incapacitated in school and career, the alarm would quickly be sounded. As it is, an estimated one tenth of all young women and one fifth of female college students are debilitated to some degree because of eating disorders.

Women happiest with their weight were found to be ten pounds underweight. Those who were at their ideal medical weight wanted to be eight pounds less.[14] A study of five hundred children found that over half of the girls regarded themselves as overweight, even though only fifteen percent actually were. Even among the ten-year-olds, thirty-one percent felt fat.[15]

Among normal weight adults, a multitude of studies indicate up to fifty-eight percent of the women and twenty-nine percent of the men perceived themselves as overweight.[16] The director of the Johns Hopkins Eating and Weight Disorders Clinic reports increasing numbers of male clients. Perhaps Wolf's fantasy may come true, but for now, all of the studies concerning weight have focused on women. One data base indicated that of thirty-six hundred studies in some way related to body image, all were about women except for one! The lone exception dealt with the correlation between better sex and improved fitness in men. The truth is, concerns about weight are found among both sexes. In a TV survey involving both men and women, forty percent reported getting fat as their greatest fear.

Female college students are particularly susceptible to problems with food, but so are gymnasts, dancers, cheerleaders, and models. Malika and her friend Rhonda, both eighteen, were busily preparing themselves a low-calorie lunch when the subject turned to boys. A fifteen minute diatribe ensued as they discussed the unfairness of having to constantly diet while their boyfriends were drinking "Pound-On" to gain weight! While most females want to be thinner, male weight concerns often involve gaining. Rather than dieting, boys are more likely to choose exercise both to lose and to build up.

When it comes to weight, men and women don't understand each other very well. People often assume that males and females differ extensively in the way they think, feel, and act toward their bodies. What differences do exist may be due to the enormous social pressures exerted on women. For example, females who eat less are perceived as being more feminine. When faced with overabundant buffet tables aboard their graduation cruiseship, Malika and her girl-friend actually lost weight because they ate only small portions of "healthy" foods in front of the boys.

Even when our perceptions of the opposite sex are accurate, they tend to be exaggerated. Men assume that women hold more negative views about their body than they actually do. Apparently, magazine editors share this belief. A survey of forty-eight men's and women's magazines reported one hundred fifty-nine articles on weight, dieting, or fitness for women compared to only thirteen for men.[17]

Author Naomi Wolf maintains that women's negative feelings about their bodies are promoted for economic and sexist reasons. Her somewhat cynical viewpoint is that a male conspiracy is at work in motivating women to purchase the goods and devices that will make them perfect. On the one hand, they are convinced that they don't measure up so they can be controlled. And on the other, that they are guilty of not living up to their beauty and fitness potential. Although Wolf has a tendency to overstate her case, one has to wonder about promoting a spray that is irritating, harmful, and expensive to combat natural vaginal odors.

Do women really view their bodies more negatively? Perhaps they just spend more time than men on grooming and health matters, although not on fitness. Such stereotyping hurts women. It suggests they worry more and do less, whereas men—who are seen as having good body images—are assumed to engage in healthier behavior.

Bob and Jenny have a college-age son and daughter. Despite a thirty-year marriage, their attitudes about their bodies are more closely in line with their same-sex child than each other. Daughter Tamara believes her current appearance is heavier than the ideal and assumes the boys on campus like thinner girls than they actually do. Jenny is frequently dieting, convinced her husband would be more attentive if she lost fifteen pounds, although he has never said anything to that effect.

Bob occasionally worries about his weight, mainly when he discovers that last year's suit doesn't fit. Son Darren is pretty happy with himself, although he has noticed the beginning of some extra flab that looks suspiciously like his dad's. Jenny is bothered by Bob's "spare tire," and the girls on campus believe Darren would be "a living doll" if he just dropped a few pounds.

What are Bob and Darren likely to do about their weight? Will they diet like the women in the house? Probably not. If anything, Darren might lift a few weights. The men have distorted their body image in a direction that fits their perception of themselves. They are consequently less motivated to tackle a serious diet plan. The women meanwhile have a distorted belief that the men in their lives want them thinner, thus driving them to search out the latest diet.[18]

Kevin is a latch-key kid. After school, he is home alone until one of his parents returns from work. He watches a lot of television. Over the last year Kevin has gained more weight than his four-foot frame can absorb. Perhaps all those ads make donuts, sugary cereal, and potato chips seem irresistible. Maybe it's the lack of exercise. Whatever the reason, children who watch a lot of TV tend to be ten percent heavier than those who don't, according to a survey reported on the television health program, *Lifeline.*

At puberty, Kevin and his friend Suzette will really begin to fret about the added pounds and inches that seem to appear out of nowhere. Suzette is likely to be especially dissatisfied because of the thinness ideal and an adolescent girl's redistribution of weight. Both will probably enjoy a more positive body image if they are involved in after school activities. Athletics are especially good for developing a sense of mastery, competence, and mood elevation. Social support promotes greater well-being. Feelings of acceptance and belonging enhance body image.[19]

Knowing all we do about the stereotyping of overweight people, sensitive intervention is called for with children.

Encouraging them to be active and involved with others is helpful. School environment can be critical. If the child perceives the school is made up of cliques which limit his or her opportunities, a change of environment may be in order. Follow-up studies with obese kids after five and ten years indicate that when parents have taken an active role in their dieting, fitness, and social interventions, weight loss is most successfully maintained. Leaving children on their own or turning them over to a psychologist is least effective.

DISTORTING THE TRUTH

Naomi Wolfe attributes her own bout with anorexia to a male classmate's poke in the stomach and admonition that "you'd better watch it." One of my husband's patients reports that weight has never been an issue for her, since she views herself as accepted for her "intelligence, strong personality, compassion, and love." But when asked what single event or circumstance did the most to help her feel good about her body, she lists losing thirty pounds. Another recalls her single most negative body image experience: the time a close male friend commented, "Why don't you take that food and just put it on your hips?" "Hips are my struggle, and this really affected me," she remembers.

Michelle is worried. Despite feeling "healthy" and "energetic" at one hundred thirty-three pounds and five feet six inches, she has developed a "complex" and believes that maybe she *should* lose weight. After all, her school thinks so. A cheerleader at a university in the East, Michelle was told she no longer had anything to cheer about since exceeding the one hundred twenty-five pound weight limit, regardless of her height.[20] No such limit exists for male cheerleaders. The school maintains their aim is to prevent injuries. Considering the number of college women with eating disorders, such solicitous concern over the possibility of a sprained ankle seems sadly misplaced.

Adolescent girls of normal weight participated in a study on body image and recent changes in poundage. Like their obese sisters, they were found to have extreme weight consciousness, lower self-esteem, and unrealistic images of their body size. Those who had recently lost weight also shared an increased risk of bizarre dieting habits and poor nutritional practices.[21]

One does not have to be fat to act fat. Being preoccupied with weight is enough.[22] Concern about appearance and fitness or dieting, by themselves, do not cause eating disorders. But being preoccupied with weight is highly correlated with perceiving the body in a distorted way. Viewing the body unrealistically is in turn connected to anorexia and bulimia.

Brenda is bulimic. Her constant concern with weight is punctuated with cycles of eating large amounts of food and getting rid of it by vomiting, using laxatives or water-elimination medications, excessive exercise, extreme dieting, missing meals, or fasting. She mistakenly believes such purging behaviors are essential for weight control. Like many bulimics, Brenda's erratic eating patterns may actually result in a slow but steady weight gain.

Gloria is anorexic. She would never lose control and binge. She seeks her thin ideal by counting calories and limiting her food selections. Believing that she is practicing good nutrition, Gloria phobically avoids "bad" foods that contain sugar, fat, or carbohydrates. Watching her weight is a full-time job requiring the same purging behaviors as the bulimic. In reality, Gloria is starving herself to poor health or death. One recalls the untimely death of the singer, Karen Carpenter, due to the side effects of a lifetime of anorexic behavior.

Whenever Gloria and Brenda stand in front of a mirror, they don't see what the world sees. Each thinks her body is far larger than it objectively is. Their ideal is one of extreme thinness. Brenda obsesses about her hips and wears only full skirts in an attempt to disguise what she only fears is there. Psychological tests indicate people like Gloria and Brenda are subject to more problems such as depression, anxiety, obsessive behaviors, and impulsivity.[23]

Becoming mildly or seriously anorexic or bulimic is frighteningly easy. All it takes is a diet adhered to a little too enthusiastically, coupled with dissatisfaction over a distorted perception in the mirror. *Control* is often the real issue. Anorexia and bulimia are maladaptive ways of dealing with life's demands.

The teen anorexic who fears the challenges of growing up seeks to maintain the asexual appearance of a little girl. The wife and mother with bulimia asks herself, "How will I manage? If I don't purge, what will I do with all those scary feelings? How will I keep from getting fat?" Such behavior continues because it becomes an addictive pattern. Not purging or eating normally generates fear and anxiety for the bulimic or anorexic, just as when the alcoholic is denied a drink.

Simply getting people to eat normally or to stop drinking is no longer the sole goal of any substance abuse therapy. Without some focus on the spiritual, emotional, and developmental needs, chances are Gloria or Brenda will simply give up their bizarre eating patterns and quickly substitute some other addictive behavior.

Marci illustrates this well. Plagued by episodes of anorexia in her past, she viewed herself as having mastered the disease. Physically stunning, Marci talked and acted like she had it together. But in truth, her addiction had simply become more socially acceptable. She carefully counted calories and monitored her diet to "eat healthy." She spent her days exercising as an aerobics instructor. By overcontrolling her body, Marci lived under the illusion that her marriage, spiritual walk, past relationships, and current relationships with her children were under control. In reality, *overcontrol is out-of-control behavior.*

The need to feel in control is addicting in itself. Marci sought validation through maintaining the perfect weight and body. While helping her feel secure and safe, her efforts left little time for deep thought about other issues in her life. Besides, these other areas were confusing and overwhelming. Overcontrol reduced her anxiety, but also required tremendous effort and constant monitoring. Maintaining her weight and figure became an obsessive focus. Weight control became the god that would save her... but the true God asks that we not be mastered by anything (1 Cor 6:12).

Marci's need to feel valuable, desirable, and loved are valid. What she thinks, believes, feels, likes, and dislikes certainly matters. Like all of us, she wants to feel safe, not lonely, cared for, and affirmed in spite of imperfections. But Marci can't *express* her needs until she *accepts* them. Most of all, she craves unconditional love... total acceptance. And she strives to get it by perfect control of her body and meeting society's standard of beauty.

Marci's real value, however, will never be met through her own efforts or the whims of society. Only a sense of wholeness will free her to establish healthy relationships with others—ones based on love and joy instead of unmet needs, fears, or what she grudgingly resents she is "supposed" to do.

"YOU CAN NEVER BE TOO RICH OR TOO THIN"

A group of women who did not suffer from eating disorders were asked to guess the size of four parts of their bodies. More than ninety-five percent of them overestimated their size, most commonly by twenty-five percent.[24] In another study, all women overestimated the width of their waist, bust, and hips, although they could estimate the size of a box accurately.[25]

Fewer men overestimate their bodies and don't seem to suffer lowered self-esteem even if they do. Seeing ourselves as larger than we are—combined with the media's slim ideal and the fact that most women will gain an average of ten pounds between twenty-five and forty-four years of age—keeps the diet gurus busy.

In a country of such abundance, why do so many Americans go to bed hungry every night? Because so many of them are on a diet! Dieting causes irritability, poor concentration, anxiety, depression, fatigue, guilt, and shame. When young girls cut out milk to save calories, their bones are weakened and they become more prone to osteoporosis later in life. Dieting makes one feel like a loser who lacks control. Although we would never starve someone we loved, we eagerly deny our own bodies the food, care, and concern necessary for healthy living. Worst of all, for most people, dieting doesn't work. Instead, it slows the metabolism, making losing weight ever more difficult.

Like the person with an eating disorder, weight control can be used to avoid painful issues in one's life. A pertinent question for anyone who is constantly dieting is, "If I weren't worried about losing weight, what problems would I be facing?" Another is, "Do I believe that changing the shape of my body will change the shape of my life?"

How we categorize ourselves is important to body image, eating behaviors, and psychological well-being. A normal weight person who thinks he or she needs to lose weight shares the same negative personal evaluation as an overweight individual. People who lose weight—but have failed to work on their negative body image—find they still struggle with leftover disapproving feelings, thoughts, and obsessive weight concerns, despite their trim shape. Increasingly, responsible weight control programs address more than learning new eating behaviors. They encourage exercising, exploring the meaning food and eating hold for the individual, and examining body image.

Research tells us that people commonly hold three views of themselves: an *actual self* (realistic), an *ideal self* (often fashioned from the media), and an *ought self* (the duty). When there are conflicts between any or all of our perceptions, rather predictable emotional distress occurs.[26]

For example, Burt's ideal self is slim and athletic. From his early years, however, his role in the family has been "the scapegoat." His niche was as an unattractive klutz and a troublemaker. Burt's ought self perversely insures his acceptance in the family. Yet the tension between that image and his ideal self causes him to sabotage remarkable achievements of weight loss and getting into shape. Emotionally, Burt is filled with agitation: feeling guilty, worried, angry, and resentful toward others.

Rita is typical of many patients my husband sees in his obstetrics-gynecology practice. After three babies in five years, she is fifty pounds overweight. The discrepancy between Rita's ideal self and her actual self results in dejection: feeling dissatisfied, discouraged, pitiful, gloomy, and frustrated with anger directed at herself.

Such constellations of emotions seriously undermine efforts to improve body image. Losing weight is frequently far more complex than declaring, "I want to be slim." People need to restructure the way they think about themselves and learn more realistic assessments. Merging the ideal and real self has been shown to be an effective way to long-lasting improvement in body image.[27]

ADVANCING FAT ACCEPTANCE

Each person has a normal weight range. "Set points" regulate metabolism and appear to be genetically influenced, along with body shape and size. But other factors can affect weight as well—such as age, activity level, hormone fluctuations, stress, alcohol, nicotine, and other drugs. We create a severe problem with body image and weight when we insist that one hundred percent of the population fit into the space on the "bell-shaped curve" occupied by the ten percent who are naturally thin.

Losing weight is hard work. Striving to maintain a weight

below a person's genetic programming becomes an obsessive battle. Little support is given for a weight that feels comfortable, is easily maintained, and is healthy—but may not match the cultural ideal. The Portland Health Institute uses small groups and individual therapy to enable people to understand negative feelings about their body image and how their attitude is influenced by our culture.[28] Their focus is, "What will make it possible so I know I deserve to be treated with affection and respect regardless of my appearance or performance."

A magazine designed for the large-sized woman is entitled *BBW*, which stands for "Big Beautiful Woman." Editor Carole Shaw writes, "This is where you STOP FEELING GUILTY about being a large-size woman and concentrate on being the beautiful and attractive PERSON you are, regardless of size."[29] Readers are reminded that they are no smarter if they reduce to size eight. In the end, no one will remember whether they took that piece of cake or not. Ads feature attractive models who are generously proportioned.

Karen reinforces the truth that healthy body image is not irrevocably tied to appearance. A size twenty-two, she maintains she feels attractive and has no problem getting boyfriends. Plenty of men prefer large women, she insists; they just don't know how to meet them. Her quarterly newsletter features well-educated and successful men who like their women big. Said one, "Simply put, a hefty gal turns me on." Another recalled, "To me a woman isn't really womanly unless she has real presence. That means she's got to be big." The newsletter began by utilizing the mailing list of the advocacy group, The National Association to Advance Fat Acceptance.

Fat or thin, people who believe they can influence their own lives have a social advantage over those who feel at the mercy of their culture and/or their significant others. A caution is in order. People who are morbidly obese—defined medically as anyone one hundred pounds or more over their ideal weight—do not have the option of simply accepting their weight. Health problems brought on by their extreme overweight dictate the need to lose a reasonable amount and medical intervention as necessary.

SELF-LOATHING AS A MOTIVATOR

You just returned from an evening at the symphony and you're miserable. You are barely in the door before you begin to loosen buttons and belts. Besides feeling stuffed into your clothes, your best friend talked all night about how she's lost twenty pounds. You hate yourself. Tomorrow you are going to call up Jenny Craig or NutriSystem or something. No more delay! Two months later the weight is off. Three months after that, the lost pounds are back again with even more!

Many factors cause rapid weight gain after dieting, but one of the big ones is a faulty impetus for losing weight in the first place. Hating the way we look is a poor motivator for losing or keeping weight off. Every bite we take reinforces our self-loathing and reminds us how far we still are from our idealized, perfect self. The body, having become a source of failure, is hated. Our fervent focus on our weight increases our anxiety and results in eating more.

The fantasized rewards never seem to materialize. We insist that we value ourselves by more than one standard, but such a belief often reflects self-denial. Denial leads to self-deception. We convince ourselves life would be good if only we weren't so heavy. Devoting our full attention to losing weight becomes justified and inner needs remain unexamined. We are too busy counting calories, keeping weight charts, and buying diet food. Perfectionists make matters worse by all-or-nothing thinking. "I am too heavy, I will never be slim. I've eaten one cookie. I'm a loser. I can never stay on a diet."

What really helps lose and keep weight off? Of course, new

and healthful ways of living are important. But of primary concern is a person's decision to affirm himself or herself as a unique, special, and valuable individual first—then setting up a program to change. Acceptance comes before long-lasting success. Thinking we will like ourselves only after reaching a particular weight goal is a sure road to defeat.

EATING ATTITUDES SURVEY*

Consider whether or not the following descriptions are true for you. If you often exhibit most of these behaviors, consult your family physician or an expert who works with eating disorders.

1. Become anxious prior to eating.
2. Am terrified about being overweight.
3. Have gone on eating binges where I feel that I may not be able to stop.
4. Feel that others pressure me to eat.
5. Feel extremely guilty after eating.
6. Am preoccupied with a desire to be thinner.
7. Exercise strenuously to burn off calories.
8. Weigh myself several times a day.
9. Think about burning up calories when I exercise.
10. Avoid foods with sugar in them.
11. Eat diet foods.
12. Feel that food controls my life.
13. Display self-control around food.
14. Engage in dieting behavior.
15. Have the impulse to vomit after meals.

* Adapted from Loma Linda University, Department of Psychiatry materials, 1982.

"IT'S THE WANTING, WE WANT—NOT THE HAVING"*

We fantasize that if we were thin and attractive, life would be different. Focusing on the desire to be thin can sometimes serve as protection from the realities of life, distracting us from the real pain and grief of living in the real world.

Take about fifteen minutes to fill out the following lists. Be specific and don't hesitate to put anything down. What happened when the wanting changed to having? Did it make you happy? Check out with some friends if getting what they wanted made them happy.

1. Things I want that I don't have:
2. Things I've wanted that I've gotten:
3. Wanting allows me to:
4. How my life would change if I got those things:
5. How my life changed when I got what I wanted:

* Adapted from *Breaking Free from Compulsive Eating* by Geneen Roth, 1984, p. 120-121.

SELF AWARENESS QUIZ II

We often continue behaviors which are not good for us even when we know they are making us and perhaps others miserable. Look beyond the obvious as you answer the following questions.

1. A problem with weight is one you would like to do without. Or would you? What are some of the benefits you get from the struggle?

2. If you no longer worried about your weight, what would you lose?

3. If you became comfortable with your weight as it is, what might you gain?

4. Do you have a regular exercise plan that is varied and reasonable?

5. You would not starve your best friend. Eating is good. Do you need to relearn how to eat when you are hungry and not feel guilty?

6. Do you eat a variety of good, nutritious foods?

7. Are you allowing the dictates of society or of someone close to you in determining what you should weigh, instead of considering a realistic balance of your personal set point, family genetics, medications, hormones, stress, and age? What weight is easy to maintain and healthy for you?*

* An excellent resource for dealing with issues of weight is *Love Hunger*, a Minirth/Meier, Thomas Nelson Publication.

7

No Perfect People

*C*INDY'S FIVE O'CLOCK ALARM shattered the early morning calm. The sun was just beginning to peek over the horizon when one well-manicured foot hit the floor, followed quickly by another. Cindy had no time to lollygag in bed! With all that needed to be done, she would barely make it to her office by eight.

Throwing the bathroom switch simultaneously turned on the lights and music. Cindy slowly peeled off the all-cotton gloves that had kept the "anti-aging softening creme" working all night on her soon-to-be-ten-years-younger hands. She quickly popped in the horseshoe-shaped plastic device filled with bleaching gel prescribed by her dentist. It was kind of uncomfortable to wear for an hour each morning, but her smile was guaranteed to be two shades whiter in a mere three weeks.

A quick glance in the mirror brought a smile to Cindy's face. Who would ever guess that a green sea-weed masque that makes you look like a monster could make you beautiful? But she was sure it was working. Those tiny lines around her lips were definitely disappearing. Just yesterday, the head of accounting had commented on how good she looked. Fifty dollars a month was a hardship, but worth every penny.

Swaying to the music, Cindy efficiently ran through a series of stretching and bending exercises. One hour later—blowdryer, hot-rollers, and make-up having accomplished their magic—the "creature" was transformed. Slipping into her tight, short mini-dress, Cindy said a prayer of thanks for the new trainer at the gym. His grueling routines had rearranged her derriere and flattened her stomach. Knowing that her mini would mean standing most of the day, Cindy groaned as she slipped into her five-inch heels. Her dismay disappeared the moment she stepped in front of her mirror. She looked terrific!

This morning was especially hurried. Cindy had an appointment for a polish change at seven. Entering the office just before eight, Cindy carefully picked up the jangling phone, frantically searching for a pencil so she wouldn't have to open a drawer and risk ruining her polish. She deftly maneuvered one to the edge of the desk where she could pick it up without breaking one of her nails—even though their length made dialing the phone difficult and necessitated a buttonhook to button her clothes.

By the end of the day—her back aching and her liquid diet shake long since expended—Cindy met with a plastic surgeon to consult on the long anticipated augmentation of her breasts. After a two-hour workout at the gym, her grueling day was finished. Hour by hour, Cindy had checked mirrors, compared herself with her officemates, and obsessed over her appearance—her mood fluctuating according to her competition and her blood sugar.

Striving for beauty can be a time-consuming, high-anxiety endeavor. A beautiful movie star lamented, "You know what it's like to walk into a room and have everyone turn and look at you? You're thinking, 'Do I have a pimple?'"

FROM VAIN TO VULGAR

The word beauty is descended from a Latin word *bellus*, meaning handsome, but derived from "bonus" or "good."

The Greek word for beauty is perhaps more accurate for someone like Cindy. *Kalos* originally referred to good looks, but over time evolved toward "morally lacking."

Beauty promises greater intimacy, satisfaction, happiness, and love—a strong motivating force in an individual's willingness to alter his or her body. In some cultures, the choice can be made for a person. Among the high-born Greeks, skull deformities achieved by binding or placing pressure on an infant's head are mentioned as far back as Hippocrates. The practice is still found in parts of Africa, Greenland, and Peru.

In other cultures, increasingly large, wooden-like saucers have been inserted in the lips. Teeth are filed or bleached to perfection among some people. The Karen women of Burma were considered beautiful if their necks were stretched by applying as many as twenty-four rings weighing as much as fifty to sixty pounds. The longest necks were unable to support the head without the rings. In Western culture, ladies' corsets served a similar function. Their tight bindings contributed to actual and psychological feelings of unsoundness and the need for support. Erect posture became a sign of high moral principles—being "straightlaced." Those who loosened their laces risked being considered "loose."

Scarification of the body has been used for tribal identification or as markers of significant lifestyle events for thousands of years. In the seventies, "Punkers" began to apply safety pins to their bodies. Today both men and women have their nipples pierced. My husband has even had patients with pierced and jeweled vulvas. Tattoos, once a symbol of the societal outcast, have gained increased status since becoming the rage among rock stars and the Hollywood crowd.

The lengths to which a person will go in mutilating and rearranging the body depend on their reference group and their status within the group. The most severe disfigurement is often among the elite. Foot binding—first introduced to give dancers a seductive sway—was adopted and practiced among the aristocracy in China for one thousand years. In order to reduce the foot to one-third its normal size, six- to eight-year-old girls had their toes bound to their sole. They were then forced to walk in progressively smaller shoes. By adulthood, their feet were completely deformed and most were unable to walk at all.

The bound foot was a symbol of luxury, refinement, and even better sex. Chinese paintings that depict lovemaking sometimes show the bandage beginning to come unwrapped, a symbol of unbounded joy and involvement. Since the husband was the only one allowed to see his wife's foot, kissing and fondling it was considered erotically appealing. Conventional wisdom suggested that the tilt of the feet created folds in the vagina that made lovemaking more enjoyable. Apparently those with foot or high heel fetishes agree.

Even more appalling is mutilation of female genitalia. The most serious type involves removal of the clitoris and labia, most commonly practiced in Arab countries like Oman, South Yemen, Domalia, Sudan, Southern Egypt, Ethiopia and Northern Kenya. Today, there are seventy-four million females from twenty countries who have suffered some degree of female clitoridectomy.[1] After the clitoris and labia are removed, the opening to the vagina is then stitched with whatever is at hand (such as thorns and thread) leaving a small hole for urine and menstrual flow. The young woman's legs are bound together to ensure the formation of scar tissue. First intercourse is extremely painful, infections and complications abound, and sexual responsiveness is reduced.

One cannot help but contemplate how most of these beautification rituals reduce a woman's competence. Consider Cindy's inability to bend over without exposing herself to the world, or run after a bus without breaking her ankle! She is light-headed from starving herself, suffers backaches, and faces economic hardship trying to pay for all this perfection. Yet these are minor when compared with the mutilation of the Arab girl's genitals.

Such extenuating procedures serve to reduce women to *ornamental beauties*. Psychologically, they render women weak and dependent on men, rather than foster a healthy inter-dependence. Confidence and self-esteem are seriously undermined by the implication that the natural way a woman is made is not good enough.

BEAUTY COMES FROM WITHIN—
WITHIN JARS, TUBES, COMPACTS

"Sexiness wears thin after awhile and beauty fades, but to be married to a man who makes you laugh everyday, ah, now that's a real treat!" So declares Joanne Woodward in reflecting on her longtime marriage to movie heartthrob Paul Newman. Women who are content with their relationships are more likely to judge themselves attractive and be more content.[2]

Studies tell us that although women have strong feelings about their appearance, aging is not the crucial factor in their body image.[3] Midlife women usually like the way they look, some even more as they age. Contrary to the stereotype of older women scurrying around in a desperate attempt to recapture their youth, they actually tend to be less self-conscious, decreasing the chance of becoming obsessed over some aspect of the body. Physical attractiveness is usually balanced by how positively a woman views herself as a person and the sense of control she feels over her life.[4]

Who has the most problems adjusting to aging? Those women who as natural or contrived beauties have chosen looks as the path of least resistance to success. Of late, a curious phenomenon influences these and other midlife women. Being "older" is finally acceptable for a woman, as long as she doesn't look it! Mature models appear frozen in time, as epitomized by Gloria Steinem, Jane Fonda, Cher, and Raquel Welch.

By the year 2000, women will make up an estimated forty-seven percent of the work force. The average woman will live to the age of eighty. First children will increasingly be born to women between the ages of thirty-five and thirty-nine.[5] The concept of midlife will drastically change. All reports indicate that the more active a person stays, the healthier he or she will be. The mere fact that there will be more older people around will affect stereotypes. In 1960, three thousand people were over one hundred. In 1980, there were thirty-two thousand. By the twenty-first century, there will be one million!

Why are our comments on body image and aging largely about women? Because a double standard exists that suggests men become more handsome, capable, and desirable with age. When it comes to men, getting old means getting better. Do men pursue youth as women reportedly do? Probably, but societal input is on their side. And, as has been true throughout their lives, men are judged by themselves and others more on what they accomplish than how they look.

THE SCALPEL AS THE NEW MASCARA

The one-page advertisement declares, "Cosmetic surgery can add happiness to your LIFE." According to the text, "When you are self-conscious about your appearance, it's difficult to express yourself freely. Cosmetic surgery can release your true beauty, allowing the joy of life to shine through you." Even though the advertisement's appeal may be exaggerated, it deals with the pertinent issue. Psychological well-being is often the main justification for cosmetic surgery.

The pressures on women to submit to surgery that is not necessary for their physical health are especially great. For example, a study conducted at the University of Toledo had both attractive and unattractive models of both sexes wear expensive, flattering clothes and ordinary-looking ones. When asked who was most appealing, the female subjects always chose the expensively dressed male, despite his looks. Male subjects always selected the prettiest model and only considered how she was dressed if asked to deliberate their choice in terms of a marriage partner.

Desirability for women tends to include surface traits, such as attractiveness, erotic ability, and sociability. Desirable traits for men tend to involve greater substance, such as achieve-ment, leadership, and job power. A good deal of what a man finds interesting in a woman is how she differs from him. Consequently, exaggerating and enhancing the intrinsic char-acteristics of one's sex becomes an important issue.

Plastic surgery is routine for those whose career demands a youthful appearance or whose physical desirability de-termines their marital résumés. In 1982, Betty Furness announced to a celebrity-filled audience that she was celebrat-ing fifty years in show business because of the skill of her plas-tic surgeon. She introduced him as the man "... who has made it possible for me to be photographed and go on work-ing." In 1990, at seventy-five, she still gave him credit for allowing her to become the oldest reporter on camera of any network.

Baby boomers have been accustomed to turning back the clock by exercise. They are now reportedly getting face-lifts in their early forties to ensure a youthful appearance throughout middle-age.[6] And for the first time, men are showing up at the plastic surgeon's office in significant num-bers. One surgeon reports that liposuction is becoming a fad among men in his community. Removal of a double chin and "love handles" quickly and with essentially no scarring holds great appeal for the man in the fast track.

Others note the increase in requests for pectoral implants to emphasize "masculine" muscularity—the latest way to look like you work out when you don't. Calf implants are popular among body builders who discover genetic limits to their ability to build up the calf proportionately. Most men undergo such surgery with the belief that it will help their careers and sex lives.

The most common surgeries in 1989 were liposuction (the spot removal of fat) and breast augmentation, both associ-ated with youthful, fit, and sexy bodies. These were followed by eyelid surgery, nose surgery, and face-lifts. Despite the risks of severe bruising, bleeding, allergic reactions, and swelling problems, seventy-one percent in a *Glamour* magazine survey reported they have had or planned to have plastic surgery.

One reason for the increased popularity in cosmetic surgery is the emphasis on "one-day" procedures. "Drop by on your day off and return to work a new you!" In the wrong hands or as a result of an individual's physiology, however, such interventions can exact a price that goes beyond the monetary value. "Facial rejuvenation" is a deep chemical peel which uses acid to eat layers of skin. Uneven pigmentation and scarring can result. Patients are particularly cautioned about the use of cosmetic laser surgery until more testing and technology is done. Lasers have been used successfully for removal of strawberry or port-wine birthmarks and tattoos.

A recently approved procedure for what has been dubbed the "receding hairline" of women is removal of veins in the legs. Up to now, removing varicosities required extensive surgery. "Sclerotherapy" has been done in Europe for forty years. In most cases, this non-invasive technique can remove sixty to ninety-five percent of the veins, with few complications and a high degree of permanence.

Collagen injections are used around eyes and for puffing up the "sad pad," the sagging skin from nose to cheek, as well as for enlarging all those sultry lips that appear to be bursting off the pages of the magazines. Although such fast procedures require little or no anesthesia, they are temporary and must be redone. Some people have allergic reactions and/or develop diseases such as rheumatoid arthritis, systemic lupus, or multiple sclerosis. Symptoms of such auto-immune diseases can be vague: malaise, flu-like symptoms, soreness of the joints.

Currently, breast implants are being carefully studied for health risks caused by leaking silicon. It is argued whether or not polyurethane-covered varieties should be replaced. Researchers are looking for links with cancer, connective tissue diseases, and rheumatoid problems. Formation of scar tissue is common in up to seventy-five percent of patients, painfully so for twenty percent. Of the more than two million women who have had breast augmentation, ninety-three percent report they were satisfied and eighty percent would do it over again, in a survey conducted by the American Society for Plastic and Reconstructive surgery.

Kelly was not interested in breast enlargement when she visited her doctor. "I hate my huge breasts. My mother was embarrassed by them and still is. That didn't help my attitude any. I never know whether men like me because of my bust or me. I feel humiliated when I walk down the street and words like "rack," "melons," and "megapuppies" drift my way. I've dieted from the time I was a little girl, hoping they would fall off. Instead, I've gotten bigger through the years. How I long to wear a tee shirt like anyone else!"

Despite some scarring, interruption of milk production, and the risk of less sensation, most women who have breast reductions are delighted with the results. These plastic surgery patients suffer the least psychological complications. This does not mean such women do not experience some grief and mourning and phantom limb sensation. Sensory changes occur in most surgery and our body image involves our kinesthetic awareness. Most patients acknowledge "something is different."

One woman deplored the feeling that her identity was eternally linked to her bra size. Another's surgery was done to correct back and shoulder pain—the most common reason for breast reduction. She also appreciated the relief of not being looked on as a sex object. Mandy's self-image was permanently affected when a persistent date commented, "You're not going to try and tell me you're a good girl with a figure like that?" So much for body image!

HARMLESS INTERVENTIONS OR SERIOUS HEALTH HAZARDS?

Michael Jackson's repeated facial surgeries keep the tabloids busy, but he is not alone in his quest for the perfect face or figure. Plastic surgery junkies abound, people who are frequently looking for a profound change in their social life and answers to real or imagined problems.[7]

People who can't get enough surgery are often psychologically disturbed. Others simply get hooked on appearing young and want to maintain the look they have achieved.

But how the individual reacts to the change in his or her body image is related to a person's developmental stage. The strongest motivating factor in seeking surgery is the desire to reduce self-consciousness, caused by heightened awareness of something about our bodies that we have labeled negatively. Mild to moderate depression is common in those seeking surgery.

For example, Willy was convinced his nose was out of proportion for his face. It was the object of his attention every time he looked in a mirror. He measured it. He compared it to every other male nose he saw. His nose made him feel inferior and left him mildly depressed. A "nose job" enabled Willy to spend time on other things. He no longer looked for signs of negativism and rejection. And, like many of his fellow patients, Willy was pleased he had finally taken the initiative and fulfilled his longstanding desire to do something about his looks.

Even with such a simple procedure, results of psychological testing show positive psychological benefits in functioning and approach to life. Follow-up studies indicate no major personality changes, but improved body image and less depression. Social relationships are changed because the individual feels more confident. The change in the way the patient reacts to others is probably the most significant factor for those who report positive outcomes of surgery. Others often seem more likable when a person is no longer so hypersensitive and preoccupied with self.

THE MAN WHO WAS DEAD

When a person reacts negatively to cosmetic surgery, it does not necessarily mean that the outcome is bad. A patient's *perception* of reality determines the psychological aftermath. This is well illustrated by a delightful fable from *Friedman's Fables,* called "The Power of Belief."

Once there was a man who announced he was dead. He skillfully parried all arguments of family and friends who tried to convince him he was not. Eventually they gave up in despair and called in outside help. A psychiatrist and an evangelist tried to convince the man he was indeed alive, but they too gave up in disgust. Finally the man's kindly and patient family physician was summoned. He asked the man, "Tell me, do dead men bleed?" "Of course not," said the man. "Then," said the doctor, "would you allow me to make a small cut in your arm, say above the elbow?" The man rolled up his sleeve.

Everyone watched as the doctor slit the flesh and blood spurted out. A round of applause went up and a sense of relief filled the room. The doctor deftly attended the wound and turned to the crowd, "Well, I hope that puts an end to this foolishness." His patient then headed for the door, with the remark, "I see I was wrong." As he turned to leave, the man added, "Dead men, in fact, do bleed."[8]

I personally experienced how *perception* affects adjustment when my breast implants (the result of a bilateral mastectomy) had to be changed. The physician did an excellent job and the results were natural and pleasing. They just weren't me! Neither were the implants he replaced, but apparently I had come to feel they were. When the doctor asked me if I was pleased, I hardly knew what to say. My mind could recognize that his work had been skillfully done, but my gut reaction did not agree.

Dissatisfied patients are often responding to the fact that others have not reacted as they expected. They may have hoped the surgery would change them into someone they like. Unrealistic goals may not have been met, such as, "If I get a face-lift, my husband won't want a divorce." The younger a person is, the more easily they adjust to procedures that have significantly altered their appearance. Perhaps older people have lived with a specific body image for a longer period of time. Older patients have an especially hard time with nose jobs, but do well with face and eye lifts that restore a look they once knew.

In the past, males requesting surgery were more likely to be disturbed before the procedure and have more difficulty adjusting afterward. Often men are embarrassed and have to deal with feelings of guilt for caring so much about their appearance. Frequently, they request subsequent operations that almost undo what they originally were convinced they wanted. Perhaps the new openness to male cosmetic surgery will lessen these reactions.

Some people find it difficult to integrate a new attractive feature into their body image, in the same way a person who has lost considerable weight sometimes still feels fat. Adjustment is a gradual process, typically requiring a year to become used to a significantly "new you." It is not unusual, for some unknown reason, that some people with the most negative first reactions adjust best in the long run.

People who request cosmetic procedures are often motivated by the desire to reduce the discrepancy between their actual and ideal self. But, body image is more than just a cosmetic concern. While surgery can't guarantee improved relationships with others, it may very well change an individual's relationship with himself or herself. Nowhere is this more true than among those patients whose reason for surgery is due to birth defects, accidents, or illness.

THE POWER OF RECONSTRUCTION

Jeremy's face was tragically misaligned. If he had been born before 1950, chances are his family would have hidden him away. Reconstructive surgery involving bone structures was not done until then. Today, Jeremy is a well-adjusted sixth grader whose look is "unusual," but not "head-turning" as it once was. Born without cheekbones, incomplete orbits for the eyes, and an underdeveloped jaw and chin, reconstructive surgery gave Jeremy a second chance.

Facial deformities cause an especially high state of anxiety. People typically become shy and retiring, often reflecting a negative self-concept. Facially deformed children tend to behave poorly in school. At first, opinion was divided about the wisdom of risking the health of children and others by using surgical intervention to improve quality of life. Today, most agree that the enrichment is worth the risk—particularly for the most common facial deformity, cleft palate.

While corrective surgery is begun soon after birth in the United States, other countries still hide away afflicted children, often subject to superstitions and mistreatment. Doctors willing to participate in medical projects to underdeveloped countries are frequently overwhelmed by the difference they can make in the outcome of a child's life. Facial deformities, for obvious reasons, have a tremendous effect on body image.

Robert Shushan, executive director of the Exceptional Children's Foundation, firmly believes that adjustment is increased and quality of life improved with appearance-altering interventions for the developmentally disabled. His goal is eliminating visual cues that call attention to mental retardation, thus giving people a better chance to demonstrate what they can do and who they really are.

Studies appear to validate this approach. For example, in Germany and Israel, surgery done to normalize the features of children with Down's Syndrome resulted in their being judged "smarter," "nicer," and "less dangerous" by teachers and peers. Since self-image is affected by how others react to us, the assumption is made that the children will be happier.

In 1990, Shushan directed a mentally retarded adult through a documented make-over that included teeth implants, new walk, modulation of the voice, hygiene, and updated clothing. Before the make-over, James Jones was known as "Wolfman" because of his missing front teeth and wild hair and beard. Although he is now able to walk down the street without causing a stir, the most significant changes in his life appear to be internal. Jones has become less combative and critical. While he still has problems, he has an exciting new sense of hope and an expectation that people will be kind to him and that he will continue to grow.[9]

DEALING WITH THE UNEXPECTED

Most people who undergo a disfiguring trauma are at first grateful to be alive. Eventually they must come to terms with what can or can't be done to restore them to normalcy. Interestingly, increasing evidence indicates that even the fatally ill tolerate and accept their situation better when procedures are done to restore their appearance. The improved quality of life seems to be crucial.

Barely into my thirties, a routine check-up revealed a breast lump. A biopsy indicated some suspicious cells but nothing warranting surgery. Within the year, however, further biopsies resulted in the decision to do a subcutaneous bilateral mastectomy—in other words, remove both breasts.

My attitude was great. I had just completed my graduate work, my son was four, and my husband and I were looking into adopting a child. Even though the mastectomy would be disfiguring, I was happy for the availability of a medical intervention that promised years of life and health. I knew that my worth as a wife and mother did not hinge on breasts. After all, I had never particularly liked my breasts. They worked adequately to nurse my son, but beyond that, they had never turned heads.

Post-surgery reality hit hard. I was scarred and ugly. Since we were overseas in the Air Force, I had received no counseling and didn't know an artificial replacement part existed. After six months, the decision would be made whether or not reconstructive surgery would be possible.

While I struggled to keep my spirits up, it seemed the rest

of the world was working equally hard to pull them down. No one was deliberately unkind. But, as is so often the case, my adjustment had as much to do with how others reacted to me as it did with what I was telling myself. Our physician friends wondered aloud if they could accept it, had it been their wives. My husband chided me for feeling sorry for myself when he caught me crying three days after the operation. In fairness, he didn't have any more help dealing with the situation than I had. I'm glad to say that he has grown to be an exceptionally sensitive and supporting husband.

Determined to remain strong, I recovered and pridefully considered turning down the opportunity for reconstruction. Finally, a sensitive friend pointed out how much simpler life would be without the hassle of a lifetime of finding special clothes, and explaining to my newly adopted daughter and others why I looked the way I did. He helped me to personally disengage from my reasonable standard for all of womankind that "breasts don't make the woman." The decision has been a good one for me. Like other women who have had breast surgery—whether as a result of mastectomy, very small breasts, or overly abundant ones—the simple act of buying clothes and lingerie without undue consideration is a true joy.

These days, reconstructive surgery is done at the time of the mastectomy or shortly afterward, if at all possible. Such immediate intervention has been shown to reduce stress, anxiety, trauma, and depression. Counseling is also helpful in improving self-esteem. A husband's affirmative attitude is related more to a woman's acceptance of her body than the degree of disfigurement. These facts attest to the truth that a positive body image can be independent of one's physical condition.

Mastectomy is but one of many disease interventions that impact body image. Hysterectomy is noted for affecting the way a woman views her femininity, even though the physiological effects of this gynecological surgery are almost totally limited to the elimination of pregnancy. Living with other long-term debilitating or disfiguring medical problems will be discussed in chapter eight.

SOMEONE ELSE'S BODY

Like others who face chronic illness, transplant candidates can be filled with anxiety, fight with depression, and suffer distorted body images. But they also face several unique issues. Some feel guilt over the knowledge that their life requires someone else's sacrifice or death. Although live donors and recipients may enjoy an increased emotional bond, donors frequently mourn the loss of their body parts after surgery. One must adjust to a new body image even if it involves an internal organ.

Although feelings about losing a body part have been studied, adjustment to adding a foreign body part is little understood. Transplant recipients and their families usually fantasize about the donor and want to know as much as possible about him or her. Counseling and the passing of time enable the patient to overcome the feeling that they have "someone else's" organ. They eventually accept it as part of themselves.

One area of speculation concerns organ "rejection" and the emotional conflicts between recipients and living donors, or concerns about the traits and life of a deceased one. Like the cannibal, some recipients fear acquiring traits of the donor. Others feel a sense of "new life"—going beyond the ability to function and having more to do with a literal new existence. The readjusted body image is also dependent on how important the patient feels the organ is. Heart recipients may consider the heart the most important organ in the body because of its alleged "emotional" attributes, as well as its physiological centrality.

Some patients suffer complications from powerful medications. Such side effects as muscle wasting, impotence, or obesity can have a significant negative impact on an individual's body image. Younger transplant recipients are especially at risk. Since drugs may cause distortion of physical features, they may look younger than their age, fail to grow at a normal rate, or have a delay in the development of secondary sexual characteristics.[10] The popular TV show, *Different Strokes,* stars kidney transplant recipient, Gary Coleman. As an adult, he is still small, cherubic looking, and reportedly most unhappy.

Unnaturally swollen, but desirous of achieving the "thin" ideal, adolescent patients make matters worse by failing to take their medication and going on debilitating diets.

THE BODY BEAUTIFUL... FOR SOME

Those of us not directly exposed to the "sport" of body building find it somewhat difficult to understand. I must confess, looking through the magazines available to the body building aficionado was an eye-opening experience in several ways. Nowhere is the old cliché truer than, "Beauty is in the eye of the beholder." Although we may begrudgingly understand a man's desire to appear super-strong and muscular, most of us still have difficulty finding beauty in a woman who can walk through dark alleys by herself!

Due to hormonal differences, a woman cannot develop muscle bulk through normal strengthening routines. Without a deliberate effort, a woman will get strong, firm, and lose some fat, but still have a soft and curvaceous appearance more traditionally associated with femininity. Serious women body builders eliminate almost all fat from their bodies. Their breasts are reduced to the underlying well-developed pectoralis muscle.

Cameo, advertised as a "complete, twenty-minute-a-day electrifying exercise guide," promises "feminine muscularity" for the nineties. But is there such a thing? Body building is a man's sport run by men. The standards for women have been modeled after that of the male... to get big. If a woman wants to be taken seriously in the sport, she must comply. Jackie Paisley, famous for her powerful back, is a contender for "Ms. Olympia," a well respected body-building contest. She advises women, that if you don't want to get as big as possible, while keeping your aesthetic quality, of course—find another sport.

And most do. Although interest in body building is burgeoning, most women are reluctant to become bigger than their male friends. Men themselves have mixed feelings about just how "hard" a "hard-body" should be. Although many admire the dedication and power of a champion female body builder, fewer find this fitness extreme someone they would like to take home... or cuddle with. Photographs accompanying articles dealing with other than muscle-building techniques—for example, sexual relationships—inevitably picture softly feminine women. Despite the stereotype of women liking the strong muscular types, the majority prefer body shapes that don't remind them of Arnold Schwarzenegger.

We can safely conclude that the motivation of the serious body builder is *not* attracting a mate. Attracting attention, maybe. Acquiring fortunes, not likely. Body builders seem challenged by how far they can push and develop their physique. Their personal body image incorporates a vision of their ideal self, maximally developed for size and strength. This goal appears to be a primary motivation.

The body builder, like the anorexic, can become very self-obsessed, albeit in a healthier direction. Some studies suggest that men who want a perfect V-shaped body are uncomfortable with their own masculinity. They hide behind a hypermasculine facade and have a much more rigid personality structure than men who care less about their shape. The verifiable psychological and physical benefits derived from a strong, healthy body are stronger motivating factors for others.

Muscle magazines rarely deal with personal and psychological issues, except as they affect training and competing Advertisements are almost solely devoted to products that promise immediate results or for specially designed clothing. "Get big NOW." "Gain Muscle, Lose Fat: At the Same Time." "What you want is what you get." "Take your next step to VICTORY." "Your search is over: BODY AMMO."

Lee Haney, "Mr. Olympia" for the last seven years, shares, "Body building has given me far more than muscles, fame, and fortune. It has given me goals and friends and taught me priceless life lessons." He speaks of discipline, a "greater source," growing up believing he could be something special, and an almost inbred enjoyment of picking up heavy things and being amazed by feats that involved strength and muscles.[11]

Lyle Alzado got far more than muscles as a result of his desire to be big and strong. A professional football player known for his size and viciousness on the field, he is dying of brain cancer. In his and many other's opinion, his rare cancer is the result of anabolic steroid use that began in 1969. Alzado wasn't big enough at less than two hundred pounds for pro football, or even a major college team. By his senior year, his oral and injected use of steroids resulted in a one hundred pound weight gain of pure muscle.

Alzado comments, "You get the feeling of being bigger than other people and stronger than other people.... It was addicting, mentally addicting. I just didn't feel strong unless I was taking something.... I couldn't stand the thought of being weak."[12] Even after retirement, he continued to use steroids and added human growth hormone. His personal life was reportedly filled with violence, he slept three or four hours a night, his cholesterol level reached four hundred, and plastic surgeons had to remove baseball-sized masses from his hip that developed from his repeated self-injections.

Today Alzado worries about fellow athletes who are so intent on being successful that they're not concerned with anything else. Too late, he grieves, "It wasn't worth it.... I went through all those wars on the football field. I was so muscular. I was a giant. Now I'm sick, and I'm scared.... When I first got out of the hospital, I felt inferior. But I don't feel inferior anymore. My strength isn't my strength anymore. My strength is my heart."[13]

Steroids are commonly available around gyms to give users a competitive edge at a potentially high price. Ben Johnson was stripped of his Olympic gold medal when testing revealed his well-chiseled body was not naturally developed. But wrestlers, football players, and body builders are most tempted to take steroids because of their sport's emphasis on "unnatural" bigness. Regular and especially long-term abusers frequently develop early heart disease. Apparently every member of a Russian championship basketball team from the late fifties died from cardiovascular complications. Ironically, while its use incites rages and extreme aggressiveness, steroids shrink the testicles. In women, they impair ovarian function.

Tragically, many athletes are skillful at "beating the tests." Since steroids are addicting, the task of getting off them is thought to be twofold. The first step is recovery from the physical withdrawal that begins within a day or two, and may last up to a week. The effect is similar to opiate withdrawal. The second step is recovery from a depressive stage that appears within a week and may last for months. The promise of actually attaining an idealized body image that seems too good to be true, is.

NEW WORRIES

As technology rockets forward, we will soon be able to determine a person's genetic propensity to disease. Such discoveries have been labeled "the diary of an individual's future." Imagine the effect on one's body image when sharing your risk for cancer or some other disease is part of dating protocol! No longer would there be a need for the line "for better or for worse" in wedding ceremonies. The "for worse" wouldn't get past the first date!

A senior researcher at the Kennedy Institute of Ethics at Georgetown University predicts genetic testing may "fundamentally change the way we see ourselves and the way others see us." The reaction of health insurers, employers, and potential mates may result in our adding one more aspect to our list of body image worries.

Modifying what fate and genes have destined for us has been helpful for some, disastrous for others. Before embarking on any program that promises a new look, the question must be asked: is what we are planning a quick fix or a solution for the wrong problem? Just as in weight loss, change directed by self-loathing will fail to provide long-lasting satisfaction.

Is the planned change to be accomplished a reasonable risk? Are the results designed to please you personally? Or is the primary goal the impact the "new you" will have on others? As many a plastic surgery patient has discovered, the reaction of others is something over which we have no control.

Learning who you are takes time. It requires letting go of images of a perfect self and societal demands. It is acknowledging that "just me" is enough. Such a concession does not necessarily preclude making changes. Realistic assessment is not the result of how we feel. The truth about who we are and the effect we have on others requires reality testing. Unexamined conclusions must be scrutinized in the light.

Nothing is wrong with taking care of ourselves. Plenty is wrong with becoming a slave to our bodies. Remember, the inevitability of aging is in our favor. Instead of becoming increasingly discontent with deteriorating bodies, the majority of people gain perspective on the way they look and its importance. Since age facilitates self-acceptance, the wisest course of action might be to wait out our discontent!

SELF AWARENESS QUIZ III
Bodies by Design

1. If you could afford to re-make your body into a perfect one, through the gym or plastic surgery, would you?

2. How would your life change if your body was "improved"?

3. Do you remember when you decided some feature about you was not OK? What were the circumstances?

4. Has the importance of having a nice body changed over the years?

5. Can you imagine yourself "growing old gracefully," or does getting old terrify you?

6. Have you ever gone to some extreme behavior, like spending too much money on clothes or not eating, in an effort to meet a standard of attractiveness you desired?

REFLECTION

If you have access to a family album, gather together pictures that reflect your growth and development over the years. Do you recall how you felt about your body at various stages of your growth and life? What patterns or consistencies can you see? Were there times when you especially disliked or felt particularly good about yourself? What were the circumstances? Pick out your favorite picture from any age and think about why you like it. Do the reasons relate to your body or what was going on in your life at the time?

Part Three

Body Image Redefined

If anything is sacred, the human body is sacred.
Walt Whitman, 1819–1892

People should be beautiful in every way—in their faces, in the way they dress, in their thoughts and in their innermost selves.
Anton Pavlovich Chekhov, 1860–1904

8

Accepting Who We Are

*A*UTHOR SKIP HOLLANDSWORTH bemoans the fate of small, plain guys growing up in world that is not always fair: "I hate hunks. They get all the attention by just standing around doing nothing. I was always at work proving myself—studying my multiplication tables, trying to be the best at the 'forward roll' during tumbling class—and everytime I finally gave myself a break, my pale body limp with exhaustion, I would spot one of these boys hanging out with his easy smile in the back of the room, casually reading the notes that the girls were passing to him."[1]

Our imperfections may be softened with humor, but their impact is not something to be dismissed as only "skin deep" or insignificant. Body image rightly belongs in the category of "serious" concerns. How we feel about ourselves affects the way we tackle life and its challenges. And how we feel about ourselves, our *self-image*, has a lot to do with body image.

Consider again the truths we have already examined:

- Positive assumptions are made about attractive people that give them an advantage.
- Negative assumptions are made about unattractive people that work against their full impact.

- The rich have an advantage because they can afford to buy the reigning stereotype.
- By kindergarten, children are playing a sometimes harsher version of the adult body image game.
- Keeping body image concerns in the forefront of our minds is big business and economically profitable.
- The young are winners and the old are losers in issues of body image.
- Women are under the greatest pressure to conform to a stereotypical standard of beauty.
- Individuals put themselves at unnecessary risk, medically and surgically, attempting to change the way they look.

CHANGING OUR WAYS

Viewed objectively, many of the standards for attractiveness can be unrealistic and unhealthy. The longing to fit in, to belong, to gain acceptance, "to be worthy of love" is a powerful incentive. The truth is, despite all our technology and personal effort, changing the external turns out to be skin deep after all. Having great teeth, even features, or reaching our goal weight offers no guarantee we will achieve our heart's desire. A good body image isn't about just being acceptable on the outside. Ultimately, we want our appearance to signal that we are valuable on the inside.

In our desire to be valuable, we unfortunately concentrate on *looking* valuable. Nothing is wrong with a desire to expand and better ourselves—as long as growth is sought for the right reasons. Frequently, attempts to improve ourselves serve as substitutes for developing genuine self-worth and personal affirmation. Focusing on self-improvement techniques can paradoxically result in self-rejection—the very opposite of what we are trying to achieve.

If we see a need to improve, it almost always stems from a sense that we are lacking in some way. While most people will argue that their motivation is simply to be the best they can be, few take the time to explore if that is really true. Preoccupation with activities that merely sound good can result in a neglected inner life which is shallow.

Ignoring aspects of ourselves we don't like and reject does not mean they go away. Instead, they have the annoying habit of finding their way to the surface—disguised as eating disorders, stomach problems, headaches, compulsive behaviors, and the like. Lots of energy can be expended trying to hide our perceived deficiencies from others and eventually from ourselves.

The discrepancy between our ideal self and our real self provides the fuel for jumping into a program or adopting a plan to become as nearly perfect as possible. Our flaws are dissected, scrutinized, and sometimes publicized, while our good points are ignored and forgotten. Fear immobilizes any thought of looking beneath the surface at what might really be wrong. Living fearfully prevents life from being joyful.

Staying the way we are may feel awful, but at least it is an *awful* we know and are comfortable living with. Getting well is scary. We must look at what we really need, who we really are, and admitting our expectations. Being realistic means we can no longer excuse ourselves on the grounds of being a victim.

TAKING STOCK

We first need to evaluate the beaten path that has become our own personal method of dealing with issues of self-acceptance. We need to set aside time to think and appraise what we have been doing. Little progress will be made without letting go—mourning—the idealized perfect self that is not you and never will be. No one enjoys doing this, which is why we keep so busy and avoid giving ourselves the time. However, our focus must shift from fantasy to that which is truly rewarding.

Begin the journey to a healthy self-image by listing the

goals you have adopted without question and question them. Study your list and acknowledge the activities you participate in that aren't working. Take all the time you need. This evaluation may require several hours, days, or weeks in order to determine what should be changed and what your new priorities are. Times of quiet seclusion enable people to remember and reevaluate.

"But," you argue, "I just took out a membership in a new fitness center, for five years!" "I spent five thousand dollars getting my face lifted!" "I've signed over my next three paychecks to a modeling school, a Dale Carnegie course, and an in-home trainer!" If such investments are not designed to fix your actual problem, you will actually be cutting your losses by eliminating them. It is never too late to do the right thing. The good news is that the solitary meditation or prayer needed to rethink your priorities is free!

TURNING TO THERAPY

What if external techniques to remake our image have not resulted in the self-fulfillment we seek? And what if we have not been able to realistically reevaluate the way we are living our lives? Then it may be appropriate to turn to more formal therapy. With the help of a trained counselor, we can find the refuge and encouragement needed to gain understanding and insight about how we are to cope with our lives.

An unhealthy focus on self-awareness can fail to nurture the connections with other people and with God that are necessary to true healing. A narcissistic view of life can lead to conflicting desires between a healthy dependence and a paranoic independence. If we avoid this danger, therapy does have its place and can be helpful.

Some problems with body image can be traced back to traumatic experiences an individual may not associate with current behavior. Some traumas have been blocked from memory. Or faulty learning may be at the core of the problem. A well qualified therapist can be enormously helpful in facilitating insight, understanding, acceptance, and healing. Many therapeutic interventions can be helpful. We will limit our discussion to those research has indicated as most helpful in dealing with issues of body image.

From the psychological standpoint, the compulsion to compare is at the heart of most problems of poor body image. A person who has body image difficulties is generally extremely self-focused. Ninety percent of what they focus on is negative. Since such people are always looking and comparing, they make the false assumption that everyone else is scrutinizing them in the same way... and their faults will never stand the test.

Therapy is helpful when it encourages such people to become aware of the words and messages they repeat to themselves and to substitute those based on reality. To illustrate, consider Leora, a recent college graduate applying for her first real job. She gets up in the morning, looks in the mirror, and exclaims, "I look awful! I should have put those tea bags on my eyes like *Cosmo* suggested! Trust me to ignore good advice! I might as well not apply for the job. I'm sure they want someone who looks alert."

Leora needs help in becoming aware of her undermining self-talk. A counselor would encourage her to make a list of when, what, and where she gives herself negative messages. Writing her self-defeating talk on paper would help Leora recognize more realistic alternatives. She could be encouraged to say instead, "I have looked better, but I have also looked worse! The people who are going to hire me are interested in more than my appearance. It's impossible to look like a prom queen every day. I'll be the best me I can be today."

Leora's tendency to exaggerate, make generalized conclusions from those exaggerations, and to ignore positives are *cognitive* errors. Such faulty thinking is the direct result of irrational thoughts, unrealistic expectations, and flawed explanations. Cognitive errors can be very wrong and lead people to decide all kinds of assessments of their body that in reality are not accurate. *Cognitive therapy* is effective in treating body-image problems because it deals with the *thoughts* a person has about the body. Those thoughts are in actuality more closely connected to the perception of the body image than with what the body actually looks like.

Clem's chronic depression is the result of his cognitive errors. He uses his emotions as a barometer for what is going on around him, which often causes him to jump to conclusions and personalize situations. For example, Clem notices his boss and a newly hired worker sharing a joke. His self-talk says, "Look at them having a great laugh. They are probably talking about how I spilled the coffee this morning. I'm so uncoordinated. I'll bet that guy gets the next promotion." Clem has nothing to base his conclusions on except his thinking errors.

The relationship between behavior and how a person thinks about his or her body is highly correlated among people who suffer from eating disorders. Almost universally, they hold extremely negative thoughts about their appearance. If therapy fails to alter this faulty thinking, the old eating patterns will likely return. Getting out of the habit of negative and self-defeating thinking is helped by asking the person to do the following:

- Pay close attention to your thoughts so patterns could be recognized that trigger negative thinking.
- Recognize the connection between faulty thinking, behavior, and how you feel.
- Explore the origin and truth of your beliefs and gather evidence to support or reject them.
- Consider the advantages and disadvantages of holding onto the beliefs.
- Institute change in the underlying rules that lead to cognitive errors.[2]

Changing the way we talk to ourselves is not a new therapy. Even Scripture mentions this approach in terms of "renewing the mind" (Rom 12:2). The recognition that how we think affects our behavior is also nothing new, "For as a man thinks within himself, so he is" (Prv 23:7, NAS). Substituting positive or realistic thoughts is a simple but effective way for a person to feel better about his or her body and its impact.

Since children fall into the same negative self-talk as adults, it is helpful to model specific, positive affirmations of their bodies and unique abilities. Generalizations—such as, "You're great"—are not very helpful. Everyone knows they are not totally great. Such generalizations offer nothing specific which can be used to refute their own negative thoughts.

REFLECTING ON OUR LOOKS

Sometimes we reinforce our tendency for negative self-talk by adding the impact of weighing ourselves or always looking at ourselves in a mirror. Continual checking augments self-consciousness. Although the problem with scales is pretty obvious, we tend to underestimate the important role mirrors play in how we think we look. Often what we see is not what is actually there. Shakespeare said it well, "Things are neither right nor wrong, but thinking makes them so." When we obsess over our reflection in the mirror, the normal can soon appear abnormal.

For some, the solution is avoiding mirrors, while others benefit from more frequent visual feedback. The possibility of using mirrors in a realistic and therapeutic way has been confirmed in numerous studies of anorexics and bulimics. Additionally, body builders incorporate mirrors to keep accurate tabs on their progress.

People who avoid mirrors are encouraged to begin with "peeks" that are slowly increased, and to couple the experience with a praise or positive affirmation of some type. Exercising in front of a mirror can give helpful feedback on posture, which says plenty about how we feel about ourselves. As we have all experienced, adjusting our posture can also change the way we feel about ourselves. Those who misuse mirrors are asked to count the number of times they look in a mirror over several days. Dividing by the number of days gives a baseline number by which progress can be measured.

A number of studies have instructed people to estimate their body size by looking in a mirror, followed by actual measurements that are then visually constructed to demonstrate discrepancies. The subjects are then asked to look again at the places that were inaccurate and repeat until there is an accurate appraisal. This experience was coupled with positive affirmations or new cognitive thoughts such as, "I am of normal weight. Many of my friends that I think are attractive weigh as much or more than I do. I think my hips are too large, but that is because I am not perceiving them correctly."

Although such an exercise may appear silly, it can be very effective. The ability to see one's body without distorting its size is a major key in the treatment of bulimia and anorexia. Distortion is a problem for many who may not fall into the category of an eating disorder, but who constantly diet and exercise or obsess over their weight.

Most of us can improve our body image by simply approaching the mirror with some affirmation about ourselves—deliberately replacing negative evaluations with positive ones. Even someone who really needs to lose weight would find this approach helps keep the mirror from becoming self-defeating. Realistic assessment can be balanced with positive feedback.

Another beneficial step is to occasionally go out without trying to look perfect. We need to learn that people really don't care, they accept us because of our sense of humor, friendliness, interest in them, and confidence in ourselves. These are the same reasons we care for them. Another activity that can be done at home is to look at old pictures to rediscover and reclaim the old self that is good. Pictures remind us of what has made us happy or sad over large periods of time. Feelings of sadness and emptiness are part of life, just as are happiness and joy. When our memories bring them up, such feelings need not be feared.

WHAT WE CAN ALL DO

Tackling a negative body image by turning to psychology is a legitimate alternative and psychologists are increasingly incorporating some form of "body work" into their therapy. All of us have the potential to improve the way we feel about our body through exercise, dance, sports, massage, and the like. Anything that uses the body to increase awareness of its boundaries, potential, and abilities can be healing.

Exercise affects our mood, self-concept, and work behavior. Its effect is not just our imagination, but something very real. Part of what we experience as a sense of well-being is due to the chemical release of endorphins, steroids, and physical relaxation. Unlike many of the solutions we have examined, exercise is safe, inexpensive, environmentally sound, and so natural that it is built right into our particular system!

Whatever the route used to get there, our goal is to get to a place where we can say with all honesty, "If this is the best I can be, it is enough." If you think you are there already, check out your conclusion by asking yourself this question: "If I was going to die in six months, would I be pursuing the same activities I'm involved in now?"

Accepting yourself is an extremely empowering experience. Speed the process along by setting modest goals instead of high-flown fantasies. Use people who are similar to you as inspiration, rather than those whose lifestyle, body type, and age do not correlate with your own.

SOCIETY'S OTHER SOLUTIONS

Psychology has increasingly recognized the importance of feelings, identity, and the body itself. Therapy certainly has its place in improving body image. We have explored in detail external solutions to issues of body image. Obviously more is involved than "Opti-fast," anti-aging cremes, and strategically placed collagen—or, in other words, meddling with aesthetics.

Education aimed at changing an individual's perception and evaluation of societal pressures and placing it in a proper perspective is important but limited. Even learning to cope with the social realities of our culture offers only a partial answer. All of these interventions have a place, but none totally produces a healthy body image. The answer must include a concept of humankind in its most generic sense.

How is a man or woman to view his or her nature, body, and other human beings? We are clearly much more than physical bodies. Judging one another in terms of passing fads of body beautiful is ludicrous, shallow, and fickle. Why are we so vulnerable to such deceptive and limited standards? Can we rise above them? Is God a necessary key to the development of a healthy body image? How does he want us to view our bodies? And what is a Christian view of the body? We will examine such questions in chapter ten.

Our goal so far has been to examine the serious impact physical appearance has on how a person lives. Some observations are simply interesting tidbits suitable for a trivia game; others make us cringe that such blatant discrimination and injustice exists. But is this simply human nature? Is this the way things have to be? Are therapy, medical interventions, reeducation, exercise, dieting, and other such efforts the best we have to offer in our struggle to form a healthy body image?

These are external solutions for an internal problem. Knowing and accepting ourselves necessitates a spiritual solution. Some external answers have proven helpful at times, unhealthy at others. They have sometimes fed our economy at the expense of truly nurturing the individual. But few of these approaches have resulted in a lasting inner peace and security.

External solutions are tenuous at best. The internal solution is one that effects a real and permanent change. Despite mind-boggling technology, an inward look provides answers to a problem that has always been with us, but that is currently reinforced by a media that is unprecedented in its power.

Before we go on to consider this spiritual solution, I want to take a brief look at people who face very serious problems with body image. Perhaps your features at least broadly measure up to what has been deemed attractive, favored, and desirable. What of the person who is severely deformed or disabled due to an accident? What profound lessons can we learn from studying their courage in the face of adversity?

9

Painful Lessons

O NCE UPON A TIME there lived a flower so gloriously beautiful that no one dared pick it. After awhile she began to wonder what could be wrong. She clearly stood higher, was more colorful, and smelled heavenly—but each time this natural beauty was passed by. The flower stretched to new heights in an effort to attract attention, but to no avail. Finally, having used all her resources, she began to droop. It was in this state that she was found by a scholarly looking man. "Just what I wanted," he said, clutching the flower to his breast. As soon as he arrived home, the man tenderly and lovingly pressed her between the pages of a book. Here, the flower's fragile beauty was admired for a long time to come.[1]

Perhaps it is not always our zenith that is most useful, appealing, and valued. In the previous chapter, we examined what we could do to feel better about ourselves. In a world that judges worth on appearance, the core issue is not how the world sees us but how we see ourselves. The bottom line is often our own insecurity about personal significance and worth.

You have been challenged to give up the idea of a perfect self and to realistically appraise who you are. Are you willing to take the necessary time to confront issues and truths about your body image? One primary issue is letting go of self-denial, particularly denial that masks our basic need and desire to be loved. Doing so enables us to look at and to own our goodness, our shortcomings, our emptiness, and our joy.

Another essential step is exploring body image from a global and spiritual perspective, which we will do in chapter ten. You may choose to give such an examination only a cursory effort. But the physically disabled must face this challenge head on if they are to live with any kind of grace. They have much to teach us about body image. In addition to their disabilities, they face the same variety of factors that influence body image, such as family support, goals, faith, and humor. Nowhere is the complexity of how a person perceives himself or herself more evident than in this special group.

Some able-bodied people despair over meeting the prevailing standards of acceptable appearance. They may battle depression, a sense of low self-worth, or anger at not fitting in. Others spend significant sums in pursuit of the exercise, diet, or fad that promises magical transformation. The majority vacillate between striving to fit the mold and trying not to think about it. All able-bodied people have a choice about what they will or won't do to meet the stereotypes of attractiveness. Most disabled men and women have no choice.

THE LARGEST MINORITY

Forty-three million disabled Americans, the nation's largest minority, often struggle to recognize their own personal worth as not dependent on being in full bloom. Many limitations are due more to a disabling environment than to physical and mental problems. A frequently hostile environment results in the highest rates of unemployment, poverty, and welfare dependency of any minority.

Work places, shopping centers, bathrooms, restaurants,

and office equipment are designed without adequate consideration of the needs of the disabled. Only of late has legislation been more actively pursued to make the world more "user friendly" to the handicapped. Even a simple trip out to dinner can become a chore. Tom Carr describes this well in the book, *Waiting Hearts*: "As I started toward the restroom, the crowded tables and chairs cut me off from a direct line to the back. Three sets of diners rose and pulled their chairs in to let me pass. When I finally got there, I stared at the door. It was a small one, probably less than twenty-four inches wide. Even my narrow wheelchair was too wide to get through."[2]

The solution has often been to segregate people with disabilities. Like people of color in the past, the handicapped have been provided separate but unequal provisions that lessen their chance of integration into society. "In an environment adapted to the needs of everyone, which appears to be both technologically and economically possible, disabled and nondisabled persons could become functionally equal; the only remaining distinction between them would be the presence of irreducible physical differences that result from labeling or visible characteristics."[3]

When the disabled can function more efficiently and productively, the rest of us may be forced to rethink the significance of body image on a person's worth. Among the able-bodied, forty-eight percent express fear that the same fate could befall them. Fifty-eight percent feel awkward or embarrassed around people who are different—especially those who are mentally ill, facially disfigured, or deaf. There is greater comfort with those who are blind or in a wheelchair.

Common prejudices about the disabled include their being "sick," mentally ill, or asexual. Such preconceptions tend to disappear with increased familiarity. It is probably a mixed blessing that seventy-four percent of able-bodied people feel pity for the disabled. Ninety-two percent admire someone striving to overcoming a handicap, according to a

1991 Harris poll.[4] Hopefully this book has challenged you to rethink your own attitude toward people who, for one reason or another, fall outside the stereotype of attractiveness.

Even with increased opportunities and familiarity, disability cannot be overlooked. Despite phrases such as "differently abled" and "physically challenged," some people are physically and/or mentally *disabled* and must learn to cope and manage. Recent efforts have been made—some good, some bad—to familiarize us with the struggles of the disabled. Movies such as *My Left Foot* and *Awakenings* have effectively dramatized the reality of coping with a handicap.

In *Regarding Henry*, an innocent trip to the store ends with a bullet in the head and a shattered life. Months of rehabilitation, a little good luck, a supportive family, and a lot of the grace of God restore Henry to his family... but as a different man. James Brady, the former White House press secretary, knows such a struggle from painful personal experience. Celebrities such as Ramon Ramos, a former NBA player, Mohammed Ali, once known as much for his quick wit as his boxing prowess, and actor Gary Busey have helped make us aware that one million Americans suffer head injuries to some degree, each year.

Although some may question her method, the first disabled woman to appear in *Playboy* graphically announced that disabled people are sexual. For the first time ever, a catalog has come to my home with a model in a wheelchair. We are slowly beginning to see the disabled as part of the mainstream.

That the disabled suffer more discrimination than most is not an arguable point. But the real purpose of taking the time to probe the lives of a few individuals is to learn from them. By what standard do they measure themselves? When the healthy and able-bodied so easily despair over perceived or real shortcomings that are miniscule by comparison, how do so many disabled not only keep going, but often live lives of inspiration and courage?

On the other hand, what factors are missing when a disabled person fails to come to terms with his or her situation? As you read the following real life stories, take note of the methods and decisions different individuals use to endure and contend with their situation. We can learn some profound lessons at the expense of someone else's pain.

LEARNING WHAT BEAUTY IS REALLY ABOUT

Dev Polymer wanted a baby... an "adorable" one. As an image consultant, her whole life revolved around beauty products. She was obsessed with her looks as though her worth depended on them. A perfect image was so important that Dev wouldn't take the garbage out without make-up and every hair in place.

Her daughter, Meredith, was born with a facial tumor, a hemangioma/lymphangioma. The tumor was so large it had distorted the facial bones and prevented her from swallowing and eating normally. Six months in the hospital and several surgeries left Meredith little improved. But by then her mother was beginning to see a little girl whose determination to live astounded everyone.

"I had invested a lifetime trying to get everyone to approve of my appearance. Now my perception of beauty was overhauled. The loveliness that radiated from my daughter when she bestowed one of her crooked little smiles outshone the most glamorous of models. All that talk of 'inner beauty' that I had once passed off as trite began to make sense."[5]

At five, Meredith endured fourteen hours of surgery to reduce the size of her overgrown face, realign her jaw, lower her left eye, and move her nose toward the center of her face. She began competing in a therapeutic horseback-riding group and entered public school, despite the difficulty of speaking with a tracheotomy. Meredith's lack of self-consciousness has contributed greatly to her acceptance by classmates. For Dev, observing her daughter's self-acceptance has freed her from "my obsession with shallow, physical perfection."

THE JOURNEY TO OVERCOME

The body is a very complex machine: a sensory register and processor; an object in space; a sense of boundary of self; and so much more. Predicting how an individual will relate to a disability is almost impossible. Good outcomes or "overcoming" a disability is measured by a person's ability to stop thinking about it all the time and get on with life. The disability is still present but not the central focus. We live in a world where body image influences jobs, friends, and status. Just how does a person cope when he or she can't play the game?

For some, it means realizing that disability is not the ultimate disaster. Health care workers, for example, can sometimes force perceptions on the handicapped with the best of intentions. "Don't build up false hope," was the message Rob Bryant received from his physical therapist when he insisted on trying to walk. His therapy became a war of what a person with his injuries could, should, and would do.

Rob refused to accept any imposed limitations. Within two years, he walked his twenty-four mile "Miracle Walk" from Dallas to Ft. Worth. His story, *Lord, Lift Me Up*, is one of overcoming through sheer hard work, drive, and an unwavering faith.[6] A powerful dream in which he saw himself crossing a finish line was seen as a spiritual promise.

Harilyn Rousso tells of resisting her mother's perceptions of how she could appear more socially acceptable:

> She made numerous attempts over the years of my childhood to have me go for physical therapy and to practice walking more "normally" at home. I vehemently refused all her efforts. She could not understand why I would not walk straight.... My disability, with my different walk and talk and my involuntary movements, having been with me

all of my life, was part of me, part of my identity. With these disability features, I felt complete and whole. My mother's attempt to change my walk, strange as it may seem, felt like an assault on myself, an incomplete acceptance of all of me, an attempt to make me over.[7]

We simply can't assume that people will react to disabilities with overwhelming despair. Consider Diane, whose life has involved many common experiences: college, dating, marriage, and divorce. "The only thing wrong with me," she states, "is that I don't have arms and legs."[8]

Remarkably, Diane's self-image is more positive than that of most people with everything intact. Her body has always felt so "normal" that she has rejected all attempts to fit her with artificial arms and legs, declaring them too heavy and restricting. In fact, Diane reports that the only time she has not felt normal was when she has worn prosthetics. Being able to get around and being independent have been more valued than looking like everyone else. Proud of her well-developed breasts, she enjoys being compared to the legendary, "Venus de Milo." Diane isn't merely "reacting" to her problems but is in control and making choices.

If an individual has a part of their body removed, one can predict that he or she will experience "phantom" limb sensations. Body image includes our sense of occupying space. Knowing how a person will respond psychologically, however, is not so easy. The truth is, many factors besides the extent of the disability are related to adjustment.

THEY SAID I'D NEVER WALK AGAIN

Unlike Diane, Barbara grew up with a strong, healthy body. A wife and mother of three teenagers, she worked hard in a busy doctor's office. Then Barbara's car was demolished by a drunken driver. Ironically, her life was saved by being pinned so tightly in the wreckage that she was prevented from bleeding to death.

The damage was extensive, requiring two resuscitations and fifteen hours of surgery. For three weeks, Barbara lay unconscious, unable to move, open her eyes, or speak. But she heard everything, including the doctors telling her father to say his goodbyes. They said if Barbara did regain consciousness, she would be a vegetable. She remembers screaming within her immobilized body, "No, Dad, don't believe them. I'm okay!"

Barbara's long recovery and rehabilitation was punctuated by her husband leaving her, having to work three jobs to care for her children, and coping with the accidental death of her youngest son. Throughout, this woman relied on her strong personal faith for support and hope.

Of all her losses, losing her sense of control was most traumatic. She believes the Lord gave that back to her with the message, "Barbara, its your choice how you react to all that has happened.... You can give up or keep fighting.... I'll be there either way." Knowing someone understood made a great difference to her. She experienced miraculous incidents of healing that were medically unexplainable.

Although there was a stage in which she hated how she looked, Barbara determined to block self-consciousness out and to concentrate instead on making a living for the kids and her own recovery. It was "one foot at a time." With the same determination and reliance on God, she returned to school seven years after the accident and completed her nursing degree while maintaining a thirty-two hour work week.

Currently, Barbara shows few outward signs of what she has been through. She works in a rehabilitation center, a job for which she is uniquely qualified. Her story, her faith, and her exuberance for life make her a woman who inspires and enriches anyone around her.

Like many women, Barbara's appearance was a priority to her before the accident. But living with crutches, braces, eye patches, and facial scarring forced her to rethink the importance of her body image. She explains:

I have learned so much through it all. I can tell you what the most important thing (besides your loved ones in life), is and I'm not being funny—the most important thing is being able to take yourself to the bathroom *by yourself,* to give yourself a shower, just to be able to take care of yourself... being independent. It's not wealth or possessions or any of that. I'm not panicked anymore by those issues. What's important is that I can walk... I walk with a limp, but I walk. I can talk, I can see, and I can work. That's what's important.[9]

THE CRISPY CRITTER

Dave Roever is a funny man. He enjoys life despite the fact that he is blind in his right eye, deaf in his right ear, his left eye doesn't blink, his hands are maimed, and most of his face is a combination of plastic surgery and prosthetic devices. He enjoys telling his audience that he plays the piano by ear, pulling his artificial ear off and pounding the keyboard gleefully.

Dave was hit by a phosphorus grenade in Vietnam. Forty percent of his flesh was burned, including half his face. Two weeks after being hit, surgeons were shocked to see him burst into flames as the phosphorus within his body ignited with the air. Dave dubbed himself the original "crispy critter."

At first he felt there was no reason to continue to live. But his young wife's faithful love supplied the courage Dave needed to keep going. Together they clung to their faith in a God who was bigger than their discouragement. Rather than feeling sorry for himself, Dave determined to laugh his troubles away. He would "look the Devil in the face and declare that greater is him that is in me, than he who is in the world."

Dave Roever was sustained by the steadfast love of God and a wife who proved he was more than his body. As a Christian speaker, he now provides laughter, comfort, and witness to many—particularly of the power to overcome extensive facial deformity.

DOUBLE DISABILITY

Possessing a healthy body image in spite of one's physical condition is usually somewhat dependent on environmental factors beyond the person's control. David, for example, grew up with a disability and a dysfunctional family. He continues his daily struggle with the reality of paraplegic spastic cerebral palsy.

When this two-pound baby was delivered in 1951, no one expected him to leave the hospital alive. David's frail life offered no hope of academic achievement, walking, or much of anything that gives life joy... or so the doctors asserted. Such a devastating prediction was unacceptable to his parents. Their son would overcome.

Despite his commitments as a pastor, David's father faithfully took him to myriad appointments, to any doctor who promised hope. For ten years, his determined mother daily orchestrated his delicate frame through two or three hours of rigorous physical therapy. He blamed her for the pain from the therapy, because he did not understand why this had to happen to him. David's first twelve years were a physical nightmare. He was categorized as "severely limited" and underwent seven surgeries.

David's mother responded to her son's very real limitations by treating them as challenges to be overcome through will power and hard work. Her own life reflected her standard of excellence and accomplishment; so would her son's. Her worth was threatened when she was unable to move David along at a pace commensurate with her effort. She dismissed the fact that her son had a severely limiting medical problem that prevented him from walking straight and tall.

By contrast, David seemed to possess an innate understanding and realistic acceptance of his limitations. This point of conflict between him and his mother was acted out in the physical therapy. It became a time of great frustration through which his mother released her pent-up emotions. David had no option but to comply.

This determination that David "overcome" was carried on in spite of the family's religious belief that illness was God's will, and God's will was not to be the object of questions or complaints. This family was not operating in a normal and healthy way. David himself was placed in a "crazymaking" situation. He was expected to go to extremes to "walk," while simultaneously accepting his condition as the divine order. This double bind has carried over into David's adult life and affected his relationships.

A conspiracy of silence permeated the household. No one was allowed to address their frustration, question why, or speak openly about the meaning and significance his disability held for each member of the family and especially for David, himself. He found it very difficult to ask for help when he genuinely needed it.

To this day, David hates to look in a mirror. He does not see a man who has surmounted tremendous odds simply by being alive, whose upper body is strong and well-developed, who can walk with crutches when it wasn't deemed possible, and who now has a master's degree after being labeled a vegetable. Instead, he sees a man filled with shame. He says, "I failed to conquer.... I'm still handicapped."

Like many people with severe disabilities, David has become somewhat reclusive since leaving school. He finds refuge in books and ideas and is striving to be published. Yet his goal is to belong and be self-sufficient. David is frustrated by society's lack of patience and insensitivity. The years of surgery, therapy, and sheer will to get around on his own left him with a walk that one of his classmates describes as "nauseating to watch." David resents people focusing on what he can't do. A young child remarked as they were working together in caring for some horses, "I'd never want to be like you, you can't do anything."

By contrast, David recalls a professor who challenged him to grow and mature. And he has. But like so many handicapped persons, David must play catch-up. He was taught little about dating and sex, and had few opportunities for normal flirting behaviors that provide the undergirding for later relationships. His social discomfort with women is due to this lack of training, plus David's belief that to a woman—as to his mother—he will never be "perfect" enough. He fights depression over unmet dreams of marriage and family.

Increasingly, David has given up hope of physical healing, but not because he has not "worked" hard enough. He has been healed of the traumatic memories of the pain at his mother's hands. He rejects those who suggest his disability is due to demon possession, lack of faith, or unconfessed or deliberate sin. Central to his belief system is that Jesus understands. To David, dignity and respect are restored for him through the Eucharist. He joyfully receives Christ's broken body, represented as broken bread, and his blood, symbolic of the pain and shame suffered. They are tangible signs that God is not against him and that the future offers wholeness (2 Cor 4:16; 5:1-5).

David's life is a good example of the complexity of factors that go into developing body image. As we look at his story, we can see that a more realistic acceptance of his condition would have led to more self-acceptance and less shame and disgust. The strides he has made have not brought the feelings of normalcy and freedom they were intended to produce, either internally or externally.

A disability is only one element of a person's life. The health of the family, financial status, educational level, plus a myriad of other factors all mold and shape our lives. Everyone has dreams and hopes and opinions. Everyone needs encouragement and opportunity. In some ways, David is well prepared to take his place in the world. In others, he is a fellow struggler. But in the end, is the world ready for him?

DEALING WITH THE PREJUDICE

A Los Angeles newscaster named Bree Walker has grown up eliminating personal barriers, only to find societal ones still very much in place. A beautiful and talented commentator, television executives hampered Bree's career by refusing to use her if viewers could see her hands. A congenital defect had left her with stub-like appendages in place of hands.

Bree's lack of self-consciousness and dogged perseverance paid off when she was finally given the chance to appear regularly on a trial basis. Viewer reaction was positive. Knowing her condition is inherited, she has nevertheless given birth to two children who share her disability. Her "so what" attitude will undoubtedly enable her children to grow up without a sense of major limitation. Having a model or someone who believes in you and your potential is critical to developing a healthy body image.

Not everyone agrees. Following the birth of her son, Bree became the subject of a call-in radio show that questioned the wisdom of becoming pregnant when there is a chance of a deformity. The show's emcee asked her listeners to comment on whether they would bring a child into the world, knowing that the child had a very good chance of having webbed hands. "I didn't say Bree Walker was wrong," she insists. "I didn't say she was immoral, I didn't say she should have an abortion. I personally think it's an unfortunate choice on her part."[10] Such an attitude is reminiscent of the involuntary sterilization of the mentally retarded once permitted in twenty-nine states.

Mara understands such prejudice and the importance of supportive and loving people. A nineteen-year-old who was born with spina bifida, Mara's enthusiasm for life is infectious. As she prepares to move into the dorm for her first year of college, she relishes being responsible for herself after years of having people take care of her.

But Mara's attitude was not always so positive. Her memories of school include mean classmates, intolerance of differences, and frequent tears. Mara's world changed in her senior year when a member of the student government volunteered to work with the handicapped students. Their friendship blossomed. "She was there for me and accepted me. She even let me scream!" And then there was her teacher who believed Mara had the potential for college. "He forced me to go to college. He pushed and expected me to do well. I know I'm capable of more and that has made me happier."

Mara's view of God was transformed as well. Before, he was a "mean and ugly monster." Now, God has become "a friend... who won't leave." In words reflective of other disabled persons I spoke with, he has promised, "I am fearfully and wonderfully made" (Ps 139). In Mara's new church, she finds acceptance. "They don't see my chair!" she declares incredulously.

Such positive support from the people around her, including her family, has been fundamental to moving on with life. Mara is still frustrated by the assumption that she is mentally handicapped because she is in a wheelchair. She speaks wistfully of a relationship with a man someday, quickly dismissing any interest in the physical aspects. "Who needs it," she says half-convincingly.

Asked if she had the chance to live life over, Mara maintains she would not necessarily change her condition. "If I weren't in this chair, I wouldn't be as sensitive a person as I am, and I'm sure I wouldn't have the endurance." With that attitude, her expressed desire to be a psychologist for the handicapped seems well chosen.

Mara describes her mother as someone who "does what needs to be done." Her mother agrees. She is uncomfortable when someone implies that taking care of Mara is a "trial" or that she is a saint. "Mara was blue at birth, but like all mothers, I asked first, 'What is it?' (I wanted a girl so badly) and only then, 'What's wrong?'"

Raising Mara to the point of independence has been challenging. She resents the fact that few doctors have addressed the emotional and spiritual impact on Mara and the family. Even though it facilitates Mara's independence, her mother is also frustrated by the fact that the wheelchair signals that Mara is sick, retarded, and asexual. It is difficult for many people to get past the stereotypes and see a person capable of caring for herself.

Mara, as well as others with severe disabilities, could easily feel like a victim. Her treatments have involved humiliating and painful procedures that have often left her feeling violated and angry. Her mother's participation in them could be seen as a breach of trust. But Mara has also been empowered by those around her. She is not bound to her wheelchair, but is freed by it. In her own words, "I'm moving on, not 'shriveling up.'"

THE NEED TO MOURN

Dave was already seated in the restaurant when I arrived, his multiple sclerosis having progressed to the point of needing an electric cart most of the time. I remembered his determination to keep walking and to walk his bride down the church aisle. Dave greeted me with his usual warmth and genuine delight. He had come a long way from the depressed and seemingly defeated man whose diagnosis was followed by the departure of his wife and two children. Dave has been able to mourn his losses.

Living with a body that no longer functions or looks good necessitates mourning. To grieve means to admit and come to terms with sadness and disappointment. Without this process of mourning, people aren't able to move on.

Moving on for Dave revolves around the word "endurance." Always a spiritual man who loves to memorize Scripture, his understanding of endurance has radically changed. It used to mean daily runs through the mountain trails of the church camp where he works. Now Dave speaks of "scriptural endurance" and "considering everything, including the seemingly 'bad' all joy" (Jas 1).

Like Mara he comments on how much more sensitive he is to the hurdles he and others face. Dave quotes from a scene in the movie, *The Princess Bride*, in which the princess is crying for true love and her attendant responds that, "Life is pain, your highness." Dave agrees with that assessment, but it is not without hope. At first, having MS meant all his expectations were dashed. His happiness was gone, his dreams of teaching the kids how to ride bikes were dashed. He had expected life to be different.

Not wanting to go through his illness and the loss of his family for no reason, Dave searched the Scripture for the truths that would enable him to endure. Gradually the thought occurred to him that the issue wasn't how his body was seen by others, but whether or not people who saw *him* saw *Christ.* Mentoring and guiding young people were never meant to produce "Dave clones," but to duplicate Christ. The condition of his body, he determined, was irrelevant.

In addition, Dave discovered a promise of restoration. Hope for a productive life was found in the biblical promise of Psalm 71:19-21:

> Your righteousness reaches the skies, O God,
> You who have done great things.
> Who, O God, is like you?
> Though you have made me see troubles, many and bitter,
> You will restore my life again;
> from the depths of the earth you will bring me up.
> You will increase my honor and comfort me once again.

Dave shares his positive perspective: "I've been restored by the discovery that I can lead people in worship.... When I was in charge of the youth I used my body to lead, now God honors me as I use my lifelong interest and love of music." Comfort has also come through the love of a beautiful woman who shares a strong love in God. Together they praise God for giving people second chances.

OVERCOMING WITH A PURPOSE

Being able to put disability aside and possess a healthy body image often seems to be bolstered by the person's having something in life they feel strongly about. "I have a passion for what I do," says Ellen MacFarlane. An award winning consumer reporter for a Florida television station, she is determined not to be slowed down by her multiple sclerosis. Pursuing her interviews in an electric scooter, she is admired for her persistence and hard work and dreaded by any who try to hoodwink the public.

Diagnosed with the worst variety of chronic-progressive MS, Ellen still says, "Sometimes a disease can be a gift. MS has changed my life in such an important way. Now I take time to smell the roses. I used to think if I could never run again, I couldn't go on. Now I know I won't run again, and I am going on."[11]

Ellen is still able to get around, but Daryl is blind and pretty much confined to his room. Still, at the age of forty-five, he says, "I've got so many goals, I want to show folks what the most severely disabled can do—all forty-one pounds of me."[12] When Daryl was getting ready to enter second grade, he developed a rash that was the precursor to a rare and usually fatal disease called dermatomyositis. Over a period of twenty years, it "gnawed away his ears, took his eyelids, then his eyes, and inched over his body, skinning him alive. It took the give from his muscles, locked his hands up under his chin and drew his knees tight against his belly."[13] Suffering intense pain, Daryl kept his mind constantly active. Sometimes he would play and replay football games in his head.

At twenty-eight, Daryl found the disease had run its course. He had his eyelids reconstructed, "So I wouldn't look so unusual and as a boost to my self-image." Since then Daryl has earned his bachelor's and master's degrees over the phone, and has a job making follow-up calls for a busy hospital. In his spare time, he and an engineer friend have developed an environmental control device that through "sipping" and "puffing" movements activates many electrical appliances for the severely disabled.

And then there's Steven Hawking, author of a book entitled *A Brief History of Time*. His progressive Lou Gehrig's disease has left him confined to a wheelchair and for the last few years, he has been unable to speak clearly or write without the aid of a specially adapted computer. This has not stopped his intellectual contributions, however. Hawking is internationally respected for his knowledge of astrophysics, the nature of time, and the universe. Some consider him the most brilliant theoretical physicist since Einstein. This man does not spend his day obsessing over his body image. "Apart from being unlucky enough to get ALS, or motor neuron disease, I have been fortunate in every other respect."[14]

JONI AND HAPPINESS

We have already seen several examples of disabled people who have not allowed the condition of their body to determine the outcome of their lives. All of them have incorporated some of the following principles into their recovery:

- Rejected the idea that not meeting societal standards of attractiveness automatically disqualifies a person from self-acceptance and happiness.
- Acknowledged that "environmental" factors outside themselves are as important to healthy adjustment as is the seriousness of their disability.
- Mourned their losses.
- Related to at least one person who believes in them and encourages them.
- Found something they feel passionately about.
- Ceased comparing themselves with others.
- Let go of bitterness and even see positives in their condition.
- Look beyond personal resources to a personal God.

Joni Eareckson Tada is another special person who has risen above her circumstances. She prizes above all the opportunity to know God better and be a powerful witness to his love and grace. Having witnessed how God has used her confinement to a wheelchair to change her from a stubborn, self-willed teenager into a young woman dependent upon his grace, Joni recognizes the value of her disability.

At the same time, Joni naturally longs to be whole again. In the meantime, she busies herself with a nonprofit ministry, "Joni and Friends," centered around giving hope and encouragement to other disabled people. Joni is an amazing woman.

Confined for two years in a rehabilitation hospital after a diving accident, she has written of the pain and despair. The road was long and tedious in "learning to be content in whatever state you are in" (Phil 4:11). She shares, "God sometimes will sacrifice outward beauty for the development of something more beautiful on the inside. It takes yielding to his will, believing that true peace and joy (which is what we're all really looking for anyway) can come no matter what one's appearance or abilities."[15]

Even though she needs full-time help from an assistant, Joni travels throughout the world working to heighten sensitivity toward the disabled. Her presentations are punctuated with songs, some of which she has composed herself. She frequently demonstrates her remarkable ability as an artist, despite having to hold her brush with her teeth.

Joni has made the transition from "why me?" to a place of personal contentment and acceptance. How did she do it? She tried a lot of things, but finds this to be her secret: "Spending time with Jesus in a personal and intimate way is the only thing that truly satisfies. Having his heart's desire become yours... wanting to be all that *he* wants you to be... longing for his affection and approval... yearning to get to know him better. When Christ becomes our emotional focus, and not just our theological or spiritual focus, our deepest longings for acceptance and approval are satisfied."[16]

A MESSAGE TO THE ABLE-BODIED

It is one thing to list characteristics and activities that enable a person to overcome adverse circumstances. It is quite another to actually see those requisites lived out in real life. The overcomers whose stories were told in chapter three share commonalities with the disabled whose lives we have just examined. To at least some degree, the majority of us have bought into deceptive and shallow standards as a way of judging ourself and others. Those who have not are often among the disabled. They have risen above the over-emphasis on the body and avoided the good-sounding but short-sighted solutions that have stunted real growth instead of nurturing it.

Those few have answered the question asked from the beginning: "Is this the way it has to be?" They respond with a resounding no! Valuing ourselves and others is possible apart from artificial and powerful societal messages. The process is assisted when the habit of comparison is discarded.

People who overcome the pressures to look and be a certain way have not avoided facing the reality of who they are. Their realistic appraisal enables them to discover and explore abilities and characteristics they can then use in unique ways. Being open to alternatives can result in many creative choices.

These people have succeeded in spite of their inability to match the ordained precepts of acceptability. They have not allowed an image of an ideal self to prevent them from looking at and owning their real selves. Sometimes quickly, sometimes over a period of time, the dream of the perfect self is mourned and released. Mourning requires tears, sadness, and facing and coming to terms with "what might have been" and "why me?" The initial sadness and despair can eventually be replaced with acceptance.

The journey is never smooth or easy. Perseverance is essential, but the passage is aided by at least one other person who believes, encourages, and sees potential. The importance of such support cannot be overlooked. The desire for relationships is the essence of our spirituality. Having been designed to care and to relate to others, our need for acceptance is primary.

Many individuals discover faith in God is a cornerstone to their well-being. But, is it an essential element before self-worth can be experienced? Some appear to function effectively without it. Others, however—like Barbara, Mara, Dave, and Joni—consider it primary. Some people do more than live successfully; they live with a lack of bitterness and an inner peace that truly surpasses all understanding (Phil 4:7).

That inner peace comes from the knowledge that one is loved and accepted, and that life has meaning and purpose beyond what appears on the six o'clock news or their personal circumstances. Those who have faced and overcome severe physical disabilities have much to teach us about this spiritual perspective.

10

The Overlooked Answer

*H*AVE YOU EVER THOUGHT HOW UNUSUAL it is to be a nation that is so technically advanced, who's people are, at the same time, returning to beliefs in archaic myths and superstitions? With technology there is an attempt to control every aspect of life; with primitive philosophies now modernized by the New Age movement, there is a desire for mystical experience with the world in a way that seeks to overcome the natural barriers and limits of material existence. We sometimes hunger for a world totally responsive to our every wish and craving—a nirvana without needs, pain, or unrelenting desires. Through technology or philosophy, we attempt to escape having to deal with limits. Acknowledging limits means accepting that sorrow, loss, aging, and death are a part of life.

Our culture is essentially narcissistic. How we are doing is no longer judged by standards based on values, belief systems, and basic truths of life. Rather than global concerns, the focus is often what is best for the individual. No wonder we are so vulnerable to the gospel of self-improvement. But this self-focus along with freedom from family ties, social organizations, and religion have not resulted in good feelings about who we are. Instead, we often feel empty.

Escape from this emptiness and insignificance is sought vicariously through the opinion of others. Using our skills and abilities, even living a life of integrity and contentment have become secondary to making a favorable impression. We are valued for how we come across, so we turn to others to determine if we are acceptable. This "indirect self-acceptance" has taken the place of measuring ourselves against world, ethical, or religious standards.

What does all this have to do with body image? Tainted by the knowledge that we have used manipulation to get it, the acknowledgment we do receive doesn't provide the boost we expected. We tell ourselves, "They wouldn't be so impressed if they knew I'm not really a blonde... had a rib removed... my nose done... or saw me in the morning!" Feeling like phonies, we escalate our standards of approval to the point of unattainable, grandiose dreams in an effort to make them count.

Yet the evidence is overwhelming: a positive self-image is not going to be realized as long as worth is measured by changeable and whimsical ideals. A sense of true worth and the resulting feeling of security occurs when we measure ourselves against time-honored truths. Spiritual grounding enables us to face the truth of who we are and to live in the real world. All societal avenues to a healthy self-image are doomed to fail, because approval ultimately depends on the unconditional affirmation of our lovability.

All the money, time, and energy spent on appearance, performance, and status can be lost under the constant pressures of rejection, criticism, introspection, guilt, fear, or anxiety. Verification of worthiness can never depend on the validation of another—even someone who loves us dearly. Instead, we give another the power to hurt and disappoint us. God remains the only reliable source of unconditional love.

Unconditional love transforms us. Being loved enables us to move from self-absorption and reach out to others. As we are freed of constantly having to prove we are somebody, we enjoy increased energy. Manipulation of friends and loved ones is no longer necessary to make ourselves feel valuable. Their intrinsic value and worth is no longer a threat. Accepting God's unconditional love makes it possible to accept mistakes and ask for forgiveness instead of working to minimize or ignore them. Most importantly, knowing our lives have significance, worth, and meaning frees us to take responsibility for our faults and to change them.

HOW DOES GOD VIEW THE BODY?

Who are we to God and how does he view the body he has designed for us? A Christian view presupposes that God is the creator of humankind. He declared what he made as being very good. Men and women are the *only* beings created in God's image and likeness. We are to be crowned with glory and honor and inherit the kingdom of God, someday even judging the angels (Heb 2:5-10; 1 Cor 6:3).

God addressed the first created human beings directly and instructed them to join together and have children. God's plan for people was that they commune with him, rule over the earth, and develop a culture that gives him glory. It is an awesome thought to accept that God cares about us and that we are special to him. Even more difficult is the fact that his affection has nothing to do with a great body or super spirituality. Yet the Bible affirms the body as the *temple* of the Holy Spirit that has been bought with a price (1 Cor 3:16-17; 1 Cor 6:19).

When God made a covenant with Abraham, he commanded that it be acknowledged through a permanent mark in the form of circumcision. The removal of the foreskin was a visual reminder of God's promise that through Abraham all the families of the earth would be blessed (Gn 12:1-2; 17:1-9). As with most symbols, its meaning slowly shifted from an outward reflection of the heart and the desire to do God's will, to an external sign of superiority.

The Old Testament story of King Saul offers additional clues as to how God looks at us as bodily creatures. When the Israelites decided they needed a king like the neighboring countries, they selected Saul. Their choice illustrates how differently man and God judge a person as qualified. Saul's qualification as king was that he was a "choice and handsome man" who was a full head and shoulders taller than his people (1 Sm 9:2). When time came for his coronation, Saul was found hiding amongst the baggage—very unkingly behavior! Yet his tendency toward melancholy was ignored because he *looked* like a king.

When God replaced Saul, he specifically instructed Samuel: "Do not look at his appearance or at the height of his stature, because I have rejected him, for God sees not as man sees, for man looks at the outward appearance, but God looks at the heart" (1 Sm 16:7). David had been eliminated from the initial screening. His family did not consider his short stature and reddish coloring "kingly" enough to bring him in from the fields. When Samuel saw him, he noticed David's "beautiful eyes and handsome appearance" in a region where dark hair and complexion was the norm. God confirmed the choice.

Does this story contradict the Bible and suggest God doesn't value the body? Not at all. The point is that *we are not valued because of what we look like.* Regular features, a great smile, and a body that runs a three-minute mile are not necessary for us to be treasured by our Creator.

WHAT DID GOD'S SON LOOK LIKE?

Did you ever wonder what Jesus looked like? I mean what he *really* looked like, not the image you had hanging in a Sunday school class, the one with the beard and those piercing, ethereal-looking blue eyes that seem to stare right past you, or the one that hung in your grandmother's hall that was actually made up of teeny-tiny words that aligned to construct the *Lord's Prayer*, or even the one that knocked your socks off when you saw it in the foyer of the Second Baptist Church. It was just like the one from Sunday School except for the black skin and piercing, dark ethereal eyes that seemed to stare right past you. Actually, the New Testament gives us few clues about what Jesus looked like. We know he was poor and from lowly Galilee.

In the prophecies of Isaiah, the Messiah was likened to a "tender shoot," perhaps suggesting delicacy, sensitivity, and gentleness. His impoverished background is poetically referred to as a "root out of parched ground." And his appearance? "He has no stately form or majesty that we should look upon him, nor appearance that we should be attracted to him" (Is 53:2-3). Jesus bucked the odds of body-image stereotyping! If you don't fit today's standards of attractiveness, you are in good company. Jesus changed human history despite his unattractive appearance and humble background.

The body of Jesus, but not his physical appearance, is of great significance. Following a gruesome crucifixion, his victory over death was celebrated in a resurrected body. Jesus was recognized by his most intimate followers at many different times and places over a period of forty days. In all, over five hundred people saw the resurrected Lord. His followers knew him by both his voice and his face (Mt 28:9; Lk 24:31). Several touched his body. For Thomas, belief was impossible without being able to feel and see the puncture wounds inflicted on the cross.

If anything proves that God values us as an amalgam of body and soul, it is the resurrection. Jesus defeated death not as a spirit or soul, but as a man of flesh and bone. He said to his disciples, "A spirit does not have flesh and bones as you see that I have" (Lk 24:39).

When God determined to relate to humankind directly, he chose to come with skin on. A fireball might have been more impressive, but Jesus came as a bodily person. His life was not one big prayer time. His growth and maturation included development of the mind and body as well. "And Jesus kept increasing in wisdom and stature, and in favor with God and men" (Lk 2:52). He ate, drank, loved, healed, and taught. In time, Jesus was raised to eternal life in a body. Bodies are not unimportant to God; bodies are essential.

AN ETERNAL PERSPECTIVE

The New Testament emphasizes the fact that Jesus rose from the dead not to die again, but to live life eternally. It's importance lies not in the fact that a dead person had been raised to life, but that Jesus was who he claimed to be: the Son of God. Jesus was the Messiah. Jesus himself had raised the dead to life, but they would die again. But Jesus was the Messiah whose death on the cross made possible reconciliation with God and eternal life for all who believe in him. Christ's sacrifice gives believers a new beginning. They are empowered by the Holy Spirit to cultivate humility, to honestly evaluate their strengths and weaknesses, to acknowledge the true source of their power, and to serve God and others (Rom 12:3).

We inherited a sinful nature from our father Adam. People need a way to be restored and unburdened from pride, shame, and guilt. Through Christ a way was made: "But he was pierced through for our transgressions, he was crushed for our iniquities; the chastening for our well-being fell upon him, and by his scourging we are healed" (Is 53:5).

Jesus' resurrection is clear evidence of the power of God to change lives. It signified that the sacrifice on the cross had been sufficient. When God looks at the believer, he sees not his sin but the perfect, unblemished account that Jesus has substituted for him. Through Jesus' death on the cross, believers become new creations that are ruled by the Holy Spirit.

Newness in Christ means surrendering our unwarranted

low self-images to God. The Holy Spirit then helps us to repair or rebuild a positive one. We gradually become more Christ-like in the way we treat ourselves and others. We begin to feel appropriate pride in the fact that our lives can make a constructive difference in this world. Paul says in 2 Corinthians 5:17 that believers are new creatures meant for an eternity with God, but they are also new creatures *now.* Believers have reason to celebrate and feel good about who they are. Renewed people can view others with high regard and not feel threatened. Acknowledging that all talents are from God creates a willingness to use them in his service.

Why do some who have been reconciled to God through Christ still live shame-based, pride-filled lives? A complete answer is beyond the scope of a book on body image. Simply put, we still live in a fallen world. The difference, however, is that Christians are no longer prisoners of sin, shortcomings, or appearances (Rom 6:15-23). Scripture promises that Christians are freed from the penalty of sin (justification), power of sin (sanctification), and presence of sin (glorification).

A person with a poor self-image concentrates on hiding any shortcomings, but God wants to give her new eyes with which to view herself more realistically—by God's standards rather than the world's standards. The Holy Spirit has been promised as a "helper" who enables Christians to bear fruit worth picking. Having a good body image is not an end in itself, but a continual series of steps that frees a person to truly love God and others.

Someday Christians are to be with Christ and receive new bodies. What will they be like? Jesus' resurrected body was clearly identifiable—complete with the wounds from the crucifixion—yet it was also changed. He was able to walk through walls and appear and disappear. The bodies of believers, too, are to be raised and changed, still reflecting individual uniqueness despite their glorified state. These resurrected bodies will be immortal, imperishable, powerful, and glorious (1 Cor 15:42-44). The destiny of a Christian is to live and reign with Christ forever (2 Tm 2:11-12; Rv 2).

HOW SHOULD WE VIEW THE BODY?

We sometimes use terms such as body, soul, and spirit when we speak of a human being. These separate divisions are just different ways of viewing the whole person. God creates humans to be a whole entity. Rather than a body with a soul, we could more accurately be called an "ensouled body" or an "embodied soul." Scripture does not teach that we are composed of higher and lower elements. It not only speaks of wholeness, it never suggests the body is "a poor relation" incapable of being considered holy (1 Thes 5:23).

Viewing the body as made up of distinct parts has tremendous consequences, the most serious being the inclination to view one part as more valuable than another. To the Christian, that almost always means elevating the spiritual side and denigrating the worth of the physical body. We present our ethereal side to God, while trying to work out our physical needs and concerns on our own. Refusing to see ourselves as a totality is one reason we so readily turn elsewhere for affirmation and validation.

The idea that body and soul are two distinct entities was a commonly held ideology originating from Greek culture. Aristotle, for example, wrote that the body was the root of the worst evil. Sins of the flesh were more despicable than sins of the spirit such as pride and jealousy. Many in the early church were influenced by Aristotle's writings. Even today, Christian behavior and attitudes can be found that have been contaminated by its concepts.

Interestingly, a dualistic theory of the body has led some to feel it can become god-like and others to reject it for its evilness. This dualism has contributed heavily to the unhealthy split of sexuality and spirituality. The Bible never teaches, for instance, that there are two kinds of love—one sensual and the other spiritual—with Satan in charge of one and God the other.

Fascination with parts instead of the whole makes it difficult to proclaim the body's larger purpose and significance. Medicine and technology sometimes boil us down to so many nuts and bolts: "Our scientists have demonstrated how water, lipids, proteins, carbohydrates, nucleic acids, and a variety of inorganic minerals are organized into an amazingly intricate system. Or more accurately... a system of systems. Those who count such things report that within each body, these raw materials are fashioned into more than seventy-five trillion cells, which in turn can be subdivided into approximately two hundred categories."[1]

Physicians are pressured to become body mechanics capable of fixing, replacing, or restoring any imperfection or annoyance. Such god-like responsibility drives some out of medicine, while spurring others on to greater intervention. Surgeon William DeVries encouraged his artificial heart transplant patient, Bill Schroeder, "Don't worry, Bill, we'll make you better than you are."

We can even intervene in the formation of a developing fetus—to exchange parts, to supply the missing chemical, to cure a mental illness, or to fashion a new set of parts to solve a sexual identity problem. As life-enhancing as such technology can be, it also contributes to confusion about the body, its wholeness, and the purpose for which it was designed.

A corpse lying at the funeral parlor has been classified as "less than meets the eye." Humans have a physical and a non-physical side and we cannot function without both. Even a prayer must be uttered with the help of the human brain. A person is fully himself or herself only in the unity of body and spirit. The combination of body and spirit together produces a whole greater than either one alone.

SEEING THE BODY AS BAD

Some people view their bodies as "animalistic" and not as precious to God as their spiritual side. For those who see them as the source of sin, bodies become a root of shame or at least ambivalence. Using the body to celebrate life, worship God, and joyfully express the glory of union with another is naturally alien to the person who perceives it as evil.

Many in our Western culture have more difficulty seeing the body as a vessel of celebration and homage. Spiritual dancing, laying on of hands for healing, bowing and kneeling, or touching for the sake of body relaxation as in massage are more common among African, Eastern Indian, Chinese, Japanese, and Jewish traditions.

The Bible says that sin originates not in the body but in the mind and heart (Rom 1:28; Jer 17:9; Mk 7:21-23; Mt 15:19). If our bodies were the problem, then maintaining strict regulation over them would clean up our act. If so, the penitents of medieval times would have been on the right track: five lashes for improper thoughts about the baker's daughter or crawling on their knees up the nearest hill for getting too exuberant in the bedroom with their spouse.

But the Bible states that harsh treatment of the body is useless for controlling or permanently changing sinful ways (Col 2:23). In the past, the "spiritual" person ran off and joined a monastery. Today's penitent is more apt to be the fellow on the elevator who chooses not to breath rather than bump into anyone, or the woman who denies herself the luxury of a hot bubble bath.

Control of the body may result in socializing only in church, limiting exposure to music, or voting down the aerobics class in the fellowship hall even though it has been re-titled, "Temple Reconstruction for Firm Believers." The attempt to eliminate anything resembling bodily pleasure often results in shutting down sexually in the bedroom as well as curtailing the Spirit in worship.

If the body was the source of sin, monitoring what might stimulate, animate, and activate it would indeed be the solution. Perhaps dismissing the body as a legitimate source of pleasure is an overreaction to the caution not to be obsessed with any physical appetite (1 Cor 6:12). The body is, after all, the mechanism by which sin works itself out.

Additionally, the Bible tells us that joining our body with someone else's is not to be taken lightly. Sexual sins *are* different from other sins (1 Cor 6:15)—somehow defiling what has been declared a "temple." Sexual union, no matter how debased, links the participants with the sacred and honored. Two people become "one flesh" when they have sex (Gn 2:24). And since they have been made in the image of God, they also—in some mysterious way—become "one flesh" in a supernatural sense. In illicit sex, the profane is joined with the holy.

The paranoia that the body is the vehicle of evil and must be denied begins with a kernel of truth. A more balanced and biblically correct perspective calls for the body to be approached with *discipline* rather than *denial.* Discipline leaves the possibility of having unpolluted, unashamed sex. Denying our natural, God-given sensations severely curtails the richness of the sexual relationship he intended. A vivid description of marital sexuality is to be found in Song of Solomon: passionate, bodily love that incorporates all five senses.

Seeing the body as the weak link to living a holy life has caused others to throw up their hands in despair. What really counts is one's spiritual intent. "I know Ol' Joe kind of likes that whiskey, but his heart is in the right place." The preacher of a large Southern church was accused of multiple adulteries. He reported to a national news magazine that he, Jimmy Swaggart, and Jim Bakker should not be expected to maintain sexual fidelity in marriage because their spiritual sincerity and commitment was what counted. Spiritual achievements, he rationalized, far outweighed what occurred in the unimportant "flesh."

On the other hand, pornographers may conceptualize the body as simply "flesh." They encourage people to experience undisciplined sensual highs, asserting that great sex can be found through the body, apart from mind and soul. Madonna, today's high-priestess of sexual license, was quoted as saying, "Everyone thinks I'm a nymphomaniac, but in bed I prefer a good book."[2] Such a statement also suggests that mind and body can be split. Truly satisfying sex results not from being free enough to practice one thousand and one positions with partners of every sex, size, and color, but from a relationship that recognizes the wholeness and value of each participant.

HOW DID "VERY GOOD" GET TO BE SO BAD?

When God created human kind in two sexes, he declared that his design was "very good." How easily that becomes interpreted as "kind of good" or "good except for sex" or "good for some but not all." When the body has been a source of pain, humiliation, and even moral and physical failure, trusting that God has wonderfully designed us becomes a challenge.

In an imperfect world, tension constantly exists between a finite and infinite perspective. The design of Adam and Eve intended relationship as its primary purpose. Tied to that was the possibility of reproduction. Adam was not to be without a companion. But just a warm body was not good enough. His partner was to be one whose *difference* was her appeal and the source of intense sexual pleasure. Eve was also meant to contribute a perspective that enriched and added to his limited view of the world. Her similarity to him was also important, for it enabled a man and woman to work together as companions with common concerns.

When Adam and Eve first inhabited Eden, they didn't have a body image problem. "They were naked and unashamed" (Gn 2:25). The first parents didn't need therapy, surgery, or body building to assure themselves of a healthy self-image. Their self-worth was the result of being in accord with God, each other, and nature. Such was the way things were originally meant to be.

When Adam and Eve disobeyed God's command as to how

they were to live within paradise, their lives changed radically. Their disobedience destroyed a harmony that men and women were to share emotionally and physically. It immediately affected the comfort with which they perceived their bodies. Extremes rather than balance came to characterize their interactions in the world.

Women became more valued for their bodies and reproductive capabilities, and less for their input on how "the earth was to be subdued." One can hardly blame women for being concerned about appearance and the ability to have a child in a world in which that was the only way they were noticed and validated. We can sympathize with the desperate pleas for pregnancy of women such as Hannah, Sarai, Rachael, and Elizabeth.

A hint of restoration to full personhood occurred when Jesus came with a message and plan of hope. But early church pastors and scholars were inevitably influenced by cultural bias against women. They ignored some important truths and bought into the prevailing attitude of a body/soul split. Women were declared to be one of two types: *Eve*, the seductress, whose body would lead men to lose their reason, spirituality, authority, and freedom; or *Mary*, the "spiritual sustainer of unsexed love."

Most of our great-great-great grandmothers and even our mothers knew to which camp they wanted to belong. Yet Jesus reminds Martha that her value lies not only in the ability to maintain a home, but in being open to spiritual truths as well—something her sister Mary already understood (Lk 10:38-42). Women were to be seen as more than their bodies or the service or produce of their bodies.

The correct balance that was to characterize relationships between men and women was upset by the Fall. In addition, the way humankind related to God also changed. Adam and Eve elevated their self-image by determining that they would decide what was right and wrong, essentially putting themselves above God.

Equally significant for our purpose, they suddenly had a sense of shame: "the eyes of both were opened, and they realized they were naked... " (Gn 3:7). The shame they felt should not be attached to the nakedness of the body. Adam and Eve had always been nude. For the first time, however, they had reason to feel *vulnerable* and *exposed*. They had defied their maker and experienced guilt. Self-image and body image plunged as a direct consequence.

Our present dilemma reflects that of Adam and Eve. Humankind continues to vacillate between sinful pride and feelings of shame and worthlessness. Some pump iron, run marathons, or resort to the surgeon's scalpel to ensure the last say on God's handiwork. This "body shop" mentality seriously affects our relationships with others. People can become so self-absorbed that a mirror becomes their best friend. The body becomes "a taut, high-tech gadget, ruled and regulated, sometimes flogged by dangerous powders and potions, and therefore less casual, less playful, less touchable, less caressable, less lovable."[3]

When the end becomes the self, taking care of ourselves can destroy us, instead of empowering us to be present to others in meaningful ways. The temptation to view our bodies as a project—especially one that at first glance appears so natural and wholesome—is tremendous. The popularity of health clubs, oat-bran, natural fibers, mountain bikes, and the hottest diet fads attest to this distorted view. With enough personal effort and discipline, our bodies—ourselves—will become powerful, even god-like.

Fit bodies are instruments to use in relationships. Our ability to speak and communicate makes us unique among God's creatures. We can relate in ways not available to all created beings. Our yearning for children and family affirms that we are not made to be self-centered. But the body chiseled out in the gym or in the operating room gives no guarantee that it will be a bearer of joy, a bridge to fellowship, a servant of others, or thus a reflection of the glory of God.

God intended us to have a "very good" self-image as created in his likeness. We were designed to live peaceably with each other, with God, with nature, and ultimately with ourselves. The perversion of that self-image into one of pride and conceit or of running ourselves down is the basic problem in living according to his design.

WHAT CAN WE DO?

What might happen to our lives, body image, and our world if we stopped viewing the body as a system or as a "part" divorced from its spiritual dimension? For one thing, we would probably reevaluate our motives and the energy directed toward self-improvement activities. If we accepted our bodies as a "gift of God," would we be healthier? Less hassled?

Would letting go of the image of the body as a private possession and understanding it instead as a part of the larger body of Christ affect the way we decide how to treat others? Would medical and physical problems be handled differently? Imagine the difference it would make if we *really* accepted that the body is created in the image of God, whether it is ugly, beautiful, able-bodied, disabled, balding, stocky, capable of pleasure and bad-breath?[4]

I invite you to begin putting into action the changes that will enable you to love yourself and others more fully. Make sure you are on a firm foundation by practicing these truths about the body and its worth:

- It is God's idea that we be "bodypersons."
- God declared that *all* his creation, including the body, was "very good."
- Each person is a *psychosomatic unity.*[5] People are to be viewed and treated in their totality, with no part being better or more holy than another.
- Sex is a gift of God for the purpose of reproduction,

pleasure, and bonding within marriage.

- God asks men and women to approach life in the body with discipline rather than denial.
- The Bible never proclaims the fleshly body as evil and the source of sin.
- The resurrection of the dead in a body of flesh is guaranteed by Jesus' resurrection.
- Because of the Fall, the image of God in humankind is "effaced" but not erased.
- Repentance from sin and acknowledgment of one's Creator results in the indwelling of the Holy Spirit and supernatural help to live in a way honoring to God.

We have discussed many of the ways we obsess and worry about external appearance. Allow yourself to take the time needed to reevaluate some of the choices you have made that are determined by the way you look. This is important if we are to overcome our tendency toward self-denial of our real pain. When we look at ourselves in the cold light of reality, we discover strengths and weaknesses. If we feel unworthy or unlovable, no amount of external fixes—no matter how doggedly applied—will bring relief. We must first become convinced that we are valuable and therefore worthy of love.

Every person on earth reflects the likeness of God. It is a high honor to be made in his image. Our worth should not be based on what is deemed significant and valuable by our society, but it should be rooted in the unconditional love and acceptance of God.

Notes

Introduction

1. "What Happened Last Week," *National Enquirer*, October 29, 1991, 21.
2. Kinder, M., *Going Nowhere Fast* (New York: Prentice Hall Press, 1990), 32. Dr. Kinder's work is insightful and inspirational in pinpointing our tendency to misplace our focus to the "outside" instead of the "inside" and in highlighting the fact that rethinking behaviors that are detrimental or unbeneficial takes time.

ONE
Beauty Is in the Eye of the Beholder

1. Blakeslee, S., "When the Mind's Mirror Is Cruel," *The New York Times*, February 7, 1991, PB1 (N), PB15 (L), Col. 1.
2. Cash, T.F., and Pruzinsky, T. (editors), *Body Images: Development, Deviance, and Change* (New York: The Guilford Press, 1990), 17.
3. Cash and Pruzinsky, 337-347.
4. Mabry, M., "Bias Begins at Home," *Newsweek*, August 5, 1991, 33.

TWO
What's Hot, What's Not

1. Dion, K., Bercheid, E., and Walster, E., "What Is Beautiful Is Good," *Journal of Personality and Social Psychology*, 1972, 24, 285.
2. Camp, J., from the book *Plastic Surgery: The Kindest Cut* (Henry Holt and Company, Inc., 1989), excerpted in *Health*, June 1989, 82.
3. Gallager, H., *FDR's Splendid Deception* (New York: Dodd, Mead, & Company, 1985).
4. Cash and Pruzinsky, 53.

5. Thomas, V., "Body-Image Satisfaction among Black Women," *Journal of Social Psychology,* February 1989, 107-112.

6. Cash and Pruzinsky, 59.

7. Cash and Pruzinsky, 55.

8. Cash and Pruzinsky, 55.

9. Sacra, C., "Mirror Images: Why an Obsession with Your Reflection May Distort the Real You," *Health Magazine,* March 1990, 22, 72.

10. Cash, T. and Trimer, C., "Sexism and Beautyism in Women's Evaluations of Peer Performance," *Sex Roles: A Journal of Research,* January 1984, 10(1-2), 89.

11. Sacra, 70-75.

12. Cash and Pruzinsky, 59.

13. Cash and Pruzinsky, 59.

14. Cash and Pruzinsky, 59.

15. Furnham, A., Hester, C., and Weir, C., "Sex Differences in the Preferences for Specific Female Body Shapes," *Sex Roles: A Journal of Research,* June 1990, 90, 743-755.

16. Furnham, et al, 745.

17. Furnham, et al, 744.

18. Cash, T., and Wunderle, J., "Self-Monitoring and Cosmetic Use among College Women," *Journal of Social Behavior and Personality,* November 1987, 2(4), 565.

19. "I Was a Cosmo Makeover," *Cosmopolitan,* July 1991, 58.

20. Cash and Pruzinsky, 60.

21. Cash, T., "Losing Hair, Losing Points? The Effects of Male Pattern Baldness on Social Impression Formation," *Journal of Applied Social Psychology,* 1990, 20, 160.

22. Cash, T., "The Psychosocial Effects of Male Pattern Balding," *Patient Care,* 1989, I (1), 22.

23. Sheldon, W.H., The Varieties of Human Physique, (New York: Harper, 1940).

24. Davis, L.L., "Perceived Somatotypes, Body-Cathexis and Attitudes towards Clothing among College Females," *Journal of Perceptual and Motor Skills,* December 1985, 61 (3, Pt 2), 1203.

25. Britton, A., "Hard Bodies, Marshmallows, and Hunks," *Marriage Partnership,* Spring 1989, 81-84.

26. Furnham, et al, 752.

27. Spillman, D.M. and Everington, C., "Somatotypes Revisited: Have the Media Changed Our Perception of the Female Body Image?," *Psychological Reports,* 1989, 64, 887-890.

28. Britton, 82-83.

29. Hallpike, C., "Social Hair," *The Body Reader* (New York: Pantheon Books, 1978), 143-144.

30. Cash and Pruzinsky, 95.
31. Cash and Pruzinsky, 54.
32. Cash and Pruzinsky, 70-75.
33. Cash and Pruzinsky, 117-118.
34. Dobson, J., "Dr. Dobson Answers Your Questions," *Focus on the Family Magazine*, August 1990, 9.
35. Rierdan, J., Koff, E., Stubbs, M., "Depressive Symptomology and Body Image in Adolescent Girls," *Journal of Early Adolescence*, 1987, 7(2), 205.
36. Elkind, D., "Teenagers Confront Mother Nature," *Parents Magazine*, May 1990, 65, 216.
37. Cash and Pruzinsky, 118.
38. Cash and Pruzinsky, 54-55.
39. Comer, J., "Building a Positive Body Image," *Parents Magazine*, November 1990, 65 (11), 235.
40. Shaw, S. and Kemeny, L., "Fitness Promotion for Adolescent Girls: The Impact and Effectiveness of Promotional Material which Emphasizes the Slim Ideal," *Adolescence*, Fall 1989, 24 (95), 685.
41. Brooks-Gunn, J., and Warren, M., "The Psychological Significance of Secondary Sexual Characteristics in Nine- to Eleven-Year-Old Girls," *Child Development*, 1988, 59, 1061.
42. Brooks-Gunn and Warren, 1065.
43. Rierdan and Stubbs, 215.
44. Gargiulo, J., Attie, I., Brooks-Gunn, J., and Warren, M., "Girls' Dating Behavior as a Function of Social Context and Maturation," *Developmental Psychology*, September 1987, 23 (5), 730-737.
45. Blyth, D., Simmons, R., Zakin, D., "Satisfaction with Body Image for Early Adolescent Females: The Impact of Pubertal Timing within Different School Environments," *Journal of Youth and Adolescence*, 1985, 14 (3), 223.
46. Aronson, E., Aronson, V., "Does a Woman's Attractiveness Influence Men's Nonsexual Reactions?" *Medical Aspects of Human Sexuality*, November 1971, 16.
47. Aronson and Aronson, 40.
48. Carli, L., study conducted at Holy Cross College, Massachusetts, 1991.
49. Satran, P., "Beauty: How Much Is It Worth in the Workplace?" *Glamour*, March 1991, 289.

THREE
The Illusive Ideal

1. Abrahams, A., and Blackman, J., "Moved by the Spirit of the Lord, Frank Peretti writes theological thrillers that sell to high heaven," *People Magazine*, June 18, 1990, 62.

2. Demaris, O., "Sylvester Stallone," *Redlands Daily Facts: Parade Magazine*, March 31, 1991, 5-6, 8.
3. "That Cosmo Girl," *Cosmopolitan*, April 1991, 66.
4. Robbins, E., "That Cosmo Girl Helen Gurley Brown," *Vis à Vis*, April 1991, 66.
5. As told in *The Betty Baxter Story* by Betty Baxter, Betty Baxter Ministries, Inc., P.O. Box 14746, Albuquerque, New Mexico, 87191, © 1985.
6. Dowd, M., "The Perils of Being Perky," *McCall's*, July 1991, 77.

FOUR
Sex Appeal

1. Johnson, J., "How to Have All the Dates You Can Handle," *Cosmopolitan*, July 1991, 104.
2. Feingold, A., "Gender Differences in the Effects of Physical Attractiveness: Testing Evolutionary Theory with Three Independent Research Domains," unpublished manuscript, Yale University, 1990.
3. Collins, N., "Demi's Big Moment," *Vanity Fair*, August 1991, 146.
4. Priscilla Bealieu Presley with Sandre Harmon, *Elvis and Me*, (New York: G.P. Putnam's Sons, 1985)
5. Pion, R., "Role of the Breast in Female Sexual Response," *Medical Aspects of Human Sexuality*, November 1975, 103-104.
6. Flesher, B., *The Sun Life* (Western Sunbathing Association, Reche Canyon, Grand Terrace, CA, 1990), 1.

FIVE
Gender in Question

1. Balcer, S., "A Restoration of the Image," *Desert Stream Ministries Newsletter*, Spring 1990, 7-8, 10.
2. Blanchard, R., and Steiner, B., *Clinical Management of Gender Identity Disorders in Children and Adults*, 1990, 10.
3. Blanchard and Steiner, 5.
4. Balcer, 8.
5. Blanchard and Steiner, 17.
6. Blanchard and Steiner, 11.
7. Jones, S., "Homosexuality According to Science," *Christianity Today*, August 1988, 29.
8. Stafford, T., "Coming Out," *Christianity Today*, August 1988, 17.
9. Blanchard and Steiner, 11.
10. Blanchard and Steiner, 56.
11. Lindgren, T., and Pauly, I., "Body Image Scale for Evaluating Transsexuals," *Archives of Sexual Behavior*, 1975, (4)(6), 649.

12. Weisel, S. "Transsexual Finds Manhood in Christ," *Los Angeles Herald-Examiner,* July 9, 1977, A7.

13. Blanchard and Steiner, 90.

14. Payne, L., *The Healing of the Homosexual* (Wheaton, Illinois: Crossway Books, 1984), 2.

15. O'Donovan, O., "Transsexualism and Christian Marriage," *Grove Booklet on Ethics No. 48* (Nottingham: Hassall & Lucking Ltd., 1982), 6.

SIX

The Battle of the Bulge

1. Wells, L., "Beyond Beauty," *Allure,* March 1991, 36.

2. "The Way We Worked Out," *Vogue,* April 1991, 216.

3. *Vogue,* 216.

4. *Vogue,* 218.

5. *Vogue,* 220.

6. Fleming, A., "Little Dolls," *Allure,* March 1991, 29.

7. Fleming, 132.

8. "Barbie Faces New Kid on the Block, the Happy to Be Me Doll," *The Sun,* August 18, 1991, D3.

9. Valle, E., editor, "The Fifty Most Beautiful People in the World," *People Extra,* Summer 1991, 8.

10. Cash and Pruzinsky, 63.

11. Miller, C., Rothblum, E., Barbour, L., Brand, P., and Felicio, D., "Social Interactions of Obese and Nonobese Women," *Journal of Personality,* June 1990, 366.

12. Miller, et al., 365-371.

13. Wolf, N., *The Beauty Myth* (New York: William Morrow and Company, Inc., 1991), 179-180.

14. Bozzi, V., "The Body in Question," *Psychology Today,* 1988, (22)(2), 10.

15. Seligman, J., Joseph, N., Donovan, J., and Gosnell, M., "The Littlest Dieters," *Newsweek,* July 1987, 48.

16. Cash and Pruzinsky, 64.

17. Cash, T., and Brown, T., "Gender and Body Images: Stereotypes and Realities," *Sex Roles,* 1989, (21)(5-6), 369.

18. Rozin, P., and Fallon, A., "Body Image, Attitudes to Weight, and Misperceptions of Figure Preference for the Opposite Sex: A Comparison of Men and Women in Two Generations," *Journal of Abnormal Psychology,* 1988, (97)(3), 342-345.

19. Richards, M., Boxer, A., Petersen, A., and Albrecht, R., "Relation of Weight to Body Image in Pubertal Girls and Boys from Two Communities," *Developmental Psychology,* 1990, (26), 319.

20. Moss, D., "Weight Limit Nothing to Cheer about," *USA Today,* August 19, 1991, 2A.

21. Fowler, B., "The Relationship of Body Image Perception and Weight Status to Recent Change in Weight Status of the Adolescent Female," *Journal of Adolescence,* 1989, (24), 560.

22. Galgan, R., Mable, H., Ouellette, T., and Balance, W., "Body Image Distortion and Weight Preoccupation in College Women," *College Student Journal,* 1989, (23)(1), 13-14.

23. Williamson, D., "Psychopathology of Eating Disorders: A Controlled Comparison of Bulimic, Obese, and Normal Subjects," *Journal of Consulting and Clinical Psychology,* 1985, (53)(2), 161.

24. Thompson, K., "Larger Than Life," *Psychology Today,* 1986, (20)(4), 38-39.

25. Bozzi, V., "The Body in Question," *Psychology Today,* 1988, (22)(2), 10.

26. Straumen, J., and Higgins, T., "Self-Discrepancies as Predictors of Vulnerability to Distinct Syndromes of Chronic Emotional Distress," *Journal of Personality,* 1988, (56), 700.

27. Butters, J., and Cash, T., "Cognitive Behavioral Treatment of Women's Body Image Dissatisfaction," *Journal of Consulting and Clinical Psychology,* 1987, (55)(6), 889-897.

28. McNichol, B., "Fat Fight: A Path to Health," *The Oregonian,* July 23, 1991, FD1, FD9.

29. Shaw, Carole, editorial, *BBW,* January 1991, 4.

SEVEN
No Perfect People

1. Cash and Pruzinsky, 103.

2. "Health News: Behavior-Romancing Body Image," *Health,* January 1990, (22)(1), 15.

3. Freedman, R., "Body Style: Time Is on Your Side," *Vogue,* April 1988, (178)(4), 177.

4. Rackley, J., Warren, S., and Bird, G., "Determinants of Body Image in Women at Midlife," *Psychological Reports,* 1988, (62), 9-10.

5. Cullerton, B., "Over Forty: Forever Young," *Bazaar,* August 1991, 59.

6. "Baby Boomers Start Skipping Middle Age," *Longevity,* May 1991, 26.

7. Conant, J., "Scalpel Slaves Just Can't Quit; Perpetual Plastic Surgery Patients Go from Face-Lift to Face-Lift in Search of Physical Perfection," *Newsweek,* January 11, 1988, 58-59.

8. Friedman, E., "The Power of Belief," *Friedman's Fables,* New York: The Guilford Press, 1990), 55-58.

9. Roark, A., "Remaking Mr. Jones," *Los Angeles Times Magazine,* October 6, 1991, 22-25, 28, 30, 46-47.

10. House, R., and Thompson, T., "Psychiatric Aspects of Organ Trans-

plantation," *The Journal of the American Medical Association,* 1988, (260)(4), 537.

11. "TotaLee Candid Haney," *Muscle and Fitness,* October 1991, 96.

12. Alzado, L., "I'm Sick and I'm Scared," *Sports Illustrated,* July 8, 1991, 20-27.

13. Alzado, L., 20-27.

EIGHT
Accepting Who We Are

1. Hollandsworth, S., "His" column in *Mademoiselle,* 1991.

2. Beck, A., *Cognitive Therapy and the Emotional Disorders* (New York: International Universities Press, 1976).

NINE
Painful Lessons

1. Friedman, "The Wallflower," 167-171.

2. Carr, G., and Carr, T., *Waiting Hearts* (Wheaton, Illinois: Harold Shaw Publishers, 1989), 101.

3. Hahn, H., "Can Disability Be Beautiful?" *Social Policy,* Winter 1988, 26.

4. Vernace, R., "Opinions about the Disabled Linked to Ignorance" *The Sun,* September 12, 1991, A7.

5. Polymer, D., "Through the Eyes of Love," *Redbook,* August 1991, 54.

6. Bryant, R., *Lord, Lift Me Up,* (Nashville: Broadman Press).

7. Rousso, H., "Fostering Healthy Self-Esteem," *The Exceptional Parent,* December 1984, 11.

8. Frank, G., "On Embodiment: A Case Study of Congenital Limb Deficiency in American Culture," *Women with Disabilities* (Philadelphia, Pennsylvania: Temple University Press, 1988), 41-71.

9. Annan, M., "They Said I'd Never Walk Again," *Modern Nurse,* Spring 1991, 16.

10. Seligman, J., and Foote, D., "Whose Baby Is This Anyway?" *Newsweek,* October 28, 1991, 73.

11. Reed, S., and Grant, M., "She Just Won't Quit," *People,* April 29, 1991, 109.

12. Frook, J., "His Mind Pulled Him Through," *Parade Magazine,* June 23, 1991, 20.

13. Frook, 20.

14. Hawking, S., *A Brief History of Time,* (Toronto, Canada: Bantam Books, 1988), vii.

15. Tada/Eareckson, J., personal correspondence.

16. Tada/Eareckson, personal correspondence.

216

TEN

The Overlooked Answer

1. Wind, J., "What Do We Do with the Body?" *Dialog*, Summer 1988, 27 (3), 192.
2. Walker, M., "Behind the Scenes," *The National Enquirer*, June 25, 1991, 12.
3. Chianese, R. "The Controlled Body," *The Humanist*, January/February 1990, 50, 9.
4. Wind, 195.
5. Hoekema, A., "How We See Ourselves," *Christianity Today*, November 1985, 30, 38.

Other Books of Interest
from Servant Publications

Verbal Abuse
Healing the Hidden Wound
Grace H. Ketterman, M.D.

Verbal Abuse explores the kinds of family systems that perpetuate abuse. Dr. Grace Ketterman explains what verbal abuse sounds like and the kind of people most likely to be abused and to become abusers. She helps readers determine if they are suffering from abuse and how to start on the road to emotional and spiritual recovery. *$14.99,* hardcover; *$8.99,* paper

Forgiving Our Parents, Forgiving Ourselves
From the Minirth-Meier Clinic
Dr. David Stoop and Dr. James Masteller

Explores the family patterns that perpetuate dysfunction. Step-by-step, readers will learn to construct a psychological family tree that will help them uncover family secrets and family habits that have profoundly shaped their adult identity.

As they develop greater understanding of their family of origin and its effect for good or ill, they will be able to take the essential step of forgiveness. When that happens, readers will find themselves moving into a place of profound spiritual healing which will change their lives forever.

$16.99, hardcover; *$12.99,* paper